TABLE OF CONTENTS

DISCLAIMER AND TERMS OF USE AGREEMENT:

(Please Read This Before Using This Book)

ideas contained in this book, you are taking full responsibility for your actions.

The authors and publisher disclaim any warranties (express or implied), merchantability, or fitness for any particular purpose. The author and publisher shall in no event be held liable to any party for any direct, indirect, punitive, special, incidental or other consequential damages arising directly or indirectly from any use of this material, which is provided "as is", and without warranties. As always, the advice of a competent legal, tax, accounting, medical or other professional should be sought where applicable.

The authors and publisher do not warrant the performance, effectiveness or applicability of any sites listed or linked to in this book. All links are for information purposes only and are not warranted for content, accuracy or any other implied or explicit purpose. No part of this may be copied, or changed in any format, or used in any way other than what is outlined within this course under any circumstances. Violators will be prosecuted.

Introduction – The Prosperity Drug

The catchy beat was disarming. I am driving down the highway with my hands tapping out the rhythm on my steering wheel. At first, I thought this was just another clever pop tune with bubblegum lyrics. Then the words to the chorus caught my attention and I began to listen...

"I don't know what's right and what's real anymore
I don't know how I'm meant to feel anymore
When we think it will all become clear
I'm being taken over by The Fear."

This song, sung by the young British pop star, Lily Allen, was not just another slickly produced tune without substance. Allen sings of the destructive impact of materialism:

"I want to be rich and I want lots of money
I want loads of clothes and loads of diamonds
I heard people die while they are trying to find them

Life's about film stars and less about mothers
It's all about fast cars and passing each other
But it doesn't matter because I'm packing plastic
and that's what makes my life so fantastic
And I am a weapon of massive consumption
and it's not my fault it's how I'm programmed to function
I don't know what's right and what's real anymore
I don't know how I'm meant to feel anymore
Cause I'm being taken over by the fear."

Among many other things, the song laments the vacuity of mindless consumption and its pervasiveness in our society. This consumption, as Allen points out, can be like any other form of addiction, providing an initial high that hooks us, but never again delivers what it promises.

Instead, it leads us down the path toward diminishing returns and never ultimately calms our fear. But fear of what?

Indeed, it is well known to students of human societies that an increase in prosperity often brings with it a precipitous decline in spiritual involvement. After all, why would anyone need a Savior when there is Master Card and Visa?

The wisest man who ever lived once said, "No servant can serve two masters; for either he will hate the one, and love the other, or else he will hold to one, and despise the other. You cannot serve God and riches"

Idolatry of the material kind easily entraps us, luring us away from faithful allegiance to God, morals, integrity and more.

In times of economic "slow down" and a sluggish economy with unemployment at an all time high, the wise man's warning seems silly. How can people be tempted to serve "the master" of money, after all, when there is so much less of it?

But the paradox of addiction is that even in money's absence, we can find our hearts soothed more by money than by anything spiritual and behold the signs of a dangerous dependence.

When our hearts find salvation and security in having more and more material gain—whether we actually hold it or not—we are reminded of "the deceitfulness of riches" and the narcotic effects of material success.

Thus clearly, the abolition of wealth or production is not the answer to materialism! Neither is taxing the rich and removing from them what they have acquired. Rather, the answer lies in the proper use of wealth in our world: as a blessing for others and not just for our own use. The wisest of men continues to counsel, "sell your possessions and give to charity; make yourselves purses which do not wear out, an unfailing treasure in heaven....For where your treasure is, there will your heart be also."

"We ought not to forbid people to be diligent and frugal: we must exhort all to gain all they can, and to save all they can. What way then can we take that our money may not sink us to the nethermost hell? There is one way, and there is no other under heaven. If those who gain all they can, and save all they can, *will likewise give all they can*, then the more they gain, the more they will grow in grace, and the more treasure they will lay up in heaven."

What is the fear? I will discuss the fear as we go along. But right now, it is most important that you understand that "To Get You Must Give!" In difficult economic times, this is far from unnecessary counsel. It may be, in fact, the very idea that finally breaks the chains of addiction and reveals a far better treasure.

The addiction is massive consumption – consumerism running rampant amongst nations and individuals. Consuming entities always lose and I will demonstrate this to you also as we go along.

In today's headlong plunge into mindless consumption, people are looking for value and worth and attempting to define themselves by what they have accumulated and own. This never ending quest for status and net worth leaves us empty on the inside. It burdens us with responsibility and silly expenses that soon become too burdensome to carry.

Today, bankruptcy filings are at an all time high. As the songs says, "Riding high in April and shot down in

May." When the crash occurs, the damage is immense; the shot to an individual's self-esteem is devastating. Families are breaking up; suicides are increasing, depression drugs are being consumed in record proportions.

Is consumerism worth it?

Is it worth the devastation and destruction it leaves behind?

But more importantly, is there a way out...a way to correct the wrong of consumerism?

We shall see...

Chapter 1 – Taken Over By the FEAR

Doubt and fear are the conscious mind's reaction to being out of control or not in control. Fear doesn't reside in our subconscious mind. I mention this fact because due to the current economic downturn in our economy, there has been much fear...a fear that has permeated throughout our society. And this fear more often than not centers on finances and money.

As a behavioral scientist for over 31-years, I have studied the human mind and why people do what they do but more importantly why people don't do what they should do. Most behavior that steps outside the "norm" of study is due to fear.

All behavior, conduct and action stems from the subconscious mind's belief systems interacting with thought. But as I have previously pointed out, fear is the conscious mind's reaction to being out of control.

It is important to point out that the conscious mind "reacts" while the subconscious mind "interacts". In any conscious mind's reaction, little or no thought is undertaken. This is what reaction is all about. If I throw a rock at your head, you "react' by instantly raising your arm to try and block it. You did sit and think about raising your arm; you reacted instinctively to protect yourself.

Fear is another instinctive reaction and when it comes to economic or financial fear, it centers upon what we call in behavioral science, "scarcity thought". Scarcity thinking is fear-based and assumes there isn't enough for everyone or that somebody else is getting your share.

Scarcity is the fundamental economic problem of having humans who have unlimited wants and needs in a world of limited resources. It states that society has insufficient productive resources to fulfill all human wants and needs. Alternatively, scarcity implies that not all of society's goals can be pursued at the same time; trade-offs are made of one good against others. In an influential 1932 essay, Lionel Robbins defined economics as "the science which studies human behavior as a relationship between ends and scarce means which have alternative uses."

In other words, for me to win, you have to lose. But here is the rub…science tells us that for every gain there is a loss and for every loss there is a gain. This statement is one that you need to ponder. Science studies the balances of many things whether they be physical such as nature or mental such as fear. But the operative word here is balance!

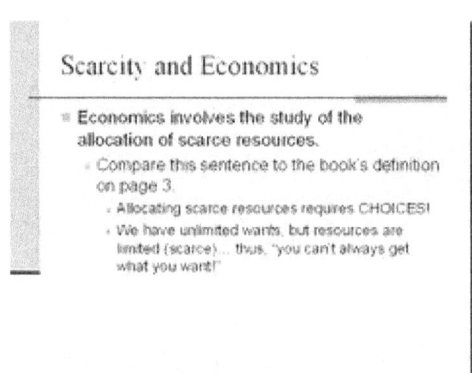

Here is a noteworthy article to consider and can be found here:
http://www.businessweek.com/the_thread/economicsunbound/archives/2007/01/should_scarcity.html

Should 'Scarcity' Be Part of the Definition of Economics?

Posted by: Michael Mandel

Every economics textbook seems to have a definition of economics right in the first chapter. And all the definitions seem to have something to do with scarcity. Here are some real examples:

12

- *"Economics is the study of choices consumers, business managers, and government official make to attain their goals, given their scarce resources.*
  "

- *"Economics is the study of how people make choices under conditions of scarcity and the results of those choices for society."*

- *"Economics is the study of how society manages its scarce resources."*

Now, I'm doing an economics textbook for McGraw-Hill, and I'm thinking about using a different definition of economics, which doesn't depend on scarcity.

Proposed definition: "Economics is the study of the functioning—and malfunctioning—of the economy, with the aim of improving living standards."

My justification for a different definition is that there are big chunks of the economy where scarcity is not important, in any but a formal sense. If anything we seem to have an abundance of food and manufactured goods, and the cost of moving and manipulating information has fallen very sharply. I'd also like to get in the sense that economics has a purpose....

The definition of economics notwithstanding, scarcity plays a very big part in any economic and/or financial model. Communism collapsed due to scarcity and only capitalism with its inherent flaws has survived. Why? Because it is built upon scarcity thought and provokes a

13

form of competition that I will leave to my readers to determine is good or bad or both.

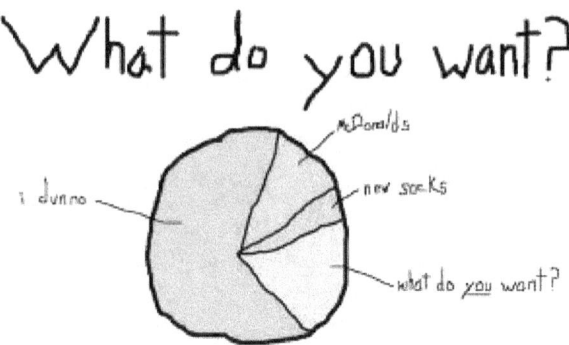

In one of my previous books I asked a question, "Do you want to have or do you want to be?" Everything I write these words I receive a ton of emails from my readers as they attempt to fully grasp what this question means.

To "consume or have" is to gain in the short term but lose in the long term as supply becomes scarce and prices climb or the "attraction" that caused you to buy wears off.

To "be" is to lose in the short term but gain in the long term. To be or "become" something you must lose something. To become a doctor you must lose part of your life to medical school, internship, and residence not to mention the cost of tuition and expenses. But in the long term, you gain a valuable profession and a good income.

Now here is something else to give careful consideration to: To a nutritionist, you are what you eat and this is true when it comes to the physiological or physical aspect of the body. But to a behavioral scientist, you are what you believe! When you eat and digest food, the food you eat is broken down and made "bio-available" to the body so that the cells of your body can use it as food. So, in essence…yes…the nutritionists are correct…you are what you eat or in other words, the food becomes YOU through the process of digestion.

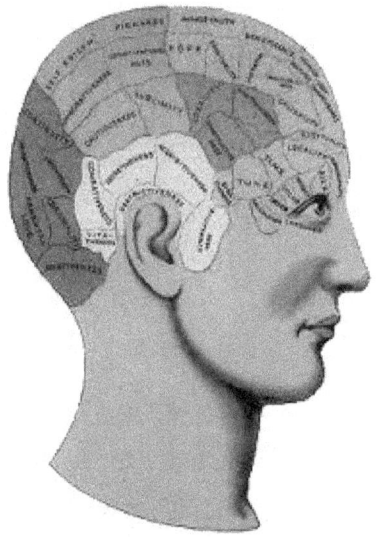

But in "mental digestion" the exact opposite is true. You take in data through your five senses and whatever you mentally digest or believe YOU become IT! This is very important especially since we live in an age where people allow others to do their thinking – i.e. the media, the internet, chat rooms, friends, family, etc.

It is easy to see how "you become it" when it comes to mental digestion. In Chapters 2-8 I am going to present a series of articles written by Henry C K Liu. He is the chairman of the New York-based Liu Investment Group and the series he presents, or more appropriately call a treatise, is titled, "The Abduction of Modernity". I want you to carefully read these articles in their entirety and then in Chapter 9 I will pull it all together for you and leave you with a composition of thought to contemplate and think about.

READ THE ARTICLES SLOWLY AND MAKE SURE YOU UNDERSTAND Mr. Liu's premises otherwise Chapter 9 will leave you in the dark. And I want you to read the articles with the conscious thought that what you mentally digest becomes you.

Chapter 2 - THE ABDUCTION OF MODERNITY Part 1: The Race Toward Barbarism

In Chapters 2-8 I am going to present a series of articles written by Henry C K Liu. He is the chairman of the New York-based Liu Investment Group and the series he presents is titled, "The Abduction of Modernity". It can be found in its entirety here at http://henryckliu.com/ along with his other writings. I promise not to leave you in the dark and I said previously, in Chapter 9 I will pull it all together for you. Note: all highlights in yellow are mine and are items I wish for you to remember. Also, I have added comments in red.

*****

The United States defines its global "war on terrorism" as a defensive effort to protect its way of life, beyond attacks from enemies with alien cultural and religious motives, to attacks from those who reject modernity itself. **This is an important point to consider; Liu is describing on a nation-entity (USA) is protecting itself from terrorism of all kinds. But the question is really, "How does an individual protect his/herself from any form of terrorism on a personal level?**

Subconsciously, as consumers, we do ont want to be told to limit our consumption or be told what we can or cannot buy and once again scarcity thought come to mind that the causes of these limitations is to deny us what is rightfully ours. This definition is derived from the views of historian Bernard Lewis, a scholar of Islamic culture at Princeton University, who traces Islamic opposition to the West beyond hostility to specific interests or actions or policies or even countries, to rejection of Western civilization for what it is. To Lewis, Western civilization stands for modernity. This anti-modernity attitude, he warns, is what lends support to the ready use of terror by Islamic fundamentalists.

Samuel Huntington in his *The Clash of Civilizations and the Remaking of World Order* argues that the collapse of the Soviet Union and the end of the Cold War will bring neither peace nor worldwide acceptance of liberal democracy. Huntington rejects Francis Fukuyama's prematurely optimistic "end of history" theme that the collapse of communism means Western civilization is destined to spread as people elsewhere seek the benefits of technology, wealth, and personal freedom it offers. Instead, because technology has been reserved for exploitation, wealth obscenely maldistributed, and freedom selectively denied to the powerless, narrow ideological conflict will transform into conflicts among people with different religions, values, ethnicities, and historical memories. These cultural factors define civilizations. Nations will increasingly base alliances on common civilization rather than common ideology; and wars will tend to occur along the fault lines between major civilizations.

Huntington points out that embracing materialist science, industrial production, technical education, rootless urbanization, and capitalistic trade does not mean the rest of the world will embrace the culture of the West. **In today's world this is called "tolerance" and it takes many forms. The so-called "enemies" of capitalism see the destructive nature of consumerism; however can offer no other working form of an economic model to take its place that doesn't smother innovation and ambition.** On the contrary, he argues that economic growth is likely to increase the aspiration for cultural sovereignty, breeding a new commitment to the values, customs, traditions, and religions of native cultures. The struggle is not capitalism against communism, but backward civilization against modern civilization.

The fault in both these views is the assumption that modernity is an exclusive characteristic of the West. On the surface, such views appear self-evident, since science and technology have been the enabling factors behind Western ascendance and dominance. But the "modern world" can be viewed as a brief aberration on the long path of human destiny, a brief period of a few centuries when narcissistic Western thinkers mistake technological development as moral progress in human civilization. Many barbaric notions, racism being the most obvious, appear under the label of modernity, rationalized by a barbaric doctrine of pseudo-science. The West takes advantage of the overwhelming power it has derived from its barbaric values to set itself up as a superior civilization. The West views its technical prowess as a predatory license for intolerance of the values and traditions of other advanced cultures.

Chinese civilization has weathered successive occupation by barbaric invaders, all of whom as rulers saw fit to adopt Chinese civilization for their own benefit and contributed to the further development of the culture they had invaded and subsequently adopted. The history of the West's interaction with the rest of the world has been culturally evangelistic, to suppress and encroach on unfamiliar cultures Westerners arbitrarily deem inferior, often based on self-satisfied ignorance. Until confronted by Western imperialism, China might have faced military conquests, but Chinese civilization had never been under attack. Barbaric invaders came to gain access to Chinese culture, not to destroy it. The West is unique in its destructive ethnocentricity. Under the domination of the West, Chinese or other non-Western intellectuals who do not speak or read Western languages are considered illiterate and ignorant, while Western "scholars", including the German philosopher Georg Wilhelm Friedrich Hegel, who do not speak or read Chinese or other non-Western languages have written erudite books on Chinese and other non-Western culture.

Gunpowder was invented around the 4th century in China by Taoist alchemist Ko Hong while seeking an elixir for immortality. It is the height of Taoist irony that the search for an elixir for immortality only yields a substance that ends life abruptly. Gunpowder would not be used in warfare in China until the 10th century, first in incendiary rockets called *feihuo* (flying fire), forerunner of today's intercontinental ballistic missiles. Explosive grenades would first be employed by armies of the Song Dynasty in 1161 against Jurchens (Nuzhen), ancestors of modern-day Manchurians.

In Chinese dynastic culture, the use of firearms in war was considered cowardly and therefore not exploited by honorable warriors of self-respect. Firearms would not develop in dynastic China, not because of the absence of know-how, but because their use had been culturally circumscribed as not being appropriate for true warriors.

In the history of human progress, willful rejection of many technological inventions is traceable to cultural preference. This is the basis for concluding that the technological militarism of the West is of barbaric roots and that a civilization built on military power remains barbaric, the reverse of modernity, notwithstanding the guise of technology.

The oldest picture in the world of a gun and a grenade is on a painted silk banner found at Dunhuang, dating to the mid-10th century that came to be in the possession of Musee Guimet in Paris in modern times. The museum on Place d'Iena was founded by French industrialist Emile Guimet, a 19th-century Asian-art collector from Lyon. On the silk banner, demons of Mara the Temptress, an evil goddess, are shown trying to harm the meditating Buddha and to distract him from his pursuit of enlightenment, with a proto-gun in the form of a fire lance and a proto-grenade in the form of a palm-size firebomb. The fact that these weapons are shown to be used only by evil demons illustrates the distasteful attitude of the ancient Chinese toward firearms.

21

Crossbows, known in Chinese as *nu,* have a shorter range than double-curved longbows and are slower in firing. But they became devastatingly accurate after a grid sight to guide their aim was invented 23 centuries ago by Prince Liu Chong of the imperial house of the Han Dynasty (206 BC-AD 220).

Crossbows were first used 28 centuries ago in the spring and Autumn Period (*Chunqiu* 770-481 BC) when their employment in the hands of the infantry neutralized the traditional superiority of war chariots. The use of crossbows thus changed the rules of warfare and the balance of power in the political landscape of ancient China, favoring those states with large *sheren* (commoner) infantry forces over those with powerful chariot-owning militant *guizu* (aristocrats).

The earliest unification of China by the Legalist Qin Dynasty (221-207 BC), whose unifying ruler was an antagonist of fragmented aristocratic feudalism, was not independent of the geopolitical impact of crossbow technology.

History records that in 209 BC, the Second Emperor (Er Shi, reigned 209-207 BC) of the Qin Dynasty, son of the unifying Qin Origin Emperor (Qin Shihuangdi, reigned 246-210 BC), who fought 26 years of continuous war to unify all under the Qin Dynasty (221-207 BC), which subsequently lasted only 14 years before collapsing, kept a crossbow regiment of 50,000 archers.

Han Dynasty historian Sima Qian, author of the classic

Records of the Historian (Shi Ji), wrote in 108 BC that a member of the Han royalty, the prince of Liang Xiao (Liang Xiao Wang), was in charge of an arsenal with several hundred thousand crossbows in 157 BC.

Two working crossbows from China, dating from the 11th century AD, one capable of repeat firing, came to be in the modern-day collection of the Simon Archery Foundation in Manchester Museum at the University of Manchester, England.

Most triggers and sights used in crossbows in China were manufactured by master craftsmen who signed their metal products with inscribed marks and dates. Shen Gua (1031-94), renowned Bei Song Dynasty (Northern Song 960-1127) scientist cum historian on Chinese science and technology, referred to his frustration over his inability to date accurately an 11th-century excavation, upon finding on a crossbow mechanism the inscription "stock by Yu Shih and bow by Chang Rou", but with no accompanying dates.

Even in 10th century BC, production of crossbows in China had already involved a sophisticated system of separation of manufacturing of parts and mass assembly of final products.

Crossbows were last used in war in China by the Qing Dynasty army in 1900, with tragic inadequacy, against the invading armies of eight allied European powers with more deadly firearms.

The ancient Greeks employed crossbows successfully at

Syracuse in 397 BC. After the fall of the Roman Empire, crossbows reappeared in Europe only after the 10th century. They were used at the Battle of Hastings in 1066 by William the Conqueror.

The Second Lateran Council of 1139 condemned crossbows, together with usury, simony (simony is the act of paying for sacraments and consequently for holy offices or for positions in the hierarchy of a church), clerical marriage and concubinage. Their use was banned under the anathema of the Church, except for use against infidels. The ban on crossbows was a position of moral righteousness yet to be taken by Christendom in modern times on the use of nuclear arms and other weapons of mass destruction.

Richard, Coeur de Lion (1157-1199), mostly absentee king of England (1189-99) and less-than-successful hero of the Crusades, took many crossbows on his Third Crusade in 1190. Hernando Cortes (1485-1547), Spanish conquistador, used the crossbow as one of his main weapons in subjugating Mexico in the 16th century.

In medieval warfare, the rules of European chivalry required, as those of dynastic Chinese martial arts did, that honorable combat be personal and bodily. Arrows were considered cowardly by medieval Europeans, as firearms were by dynastic Chinese up to the 19th century. The use of bows and arrows was stooped to only by those outside of the socio-military establishment, the likes of outlawed English yeomen of the 12th century, such as Robin Hood and his chief archer, Little John, legendary folk heroes of English ballads. Another famous 13th-century archer was the legendary Swiss patriot William Tell, whose story would be made popular by Friedrich von Schiller's drama and later by Gioacchino Antonio Rossini's popular opera.

European knights, when prepared to suffer calculated losses, were able to survive slow-firing enemy crossbows with limited range. In sufficient numbers, the horsemen were able to decimate in full gallop an unprotected line of much-despised enemy crossbow-men. However, they were not able to overcome fast-firing longbows with long range.

Two millennia after the invention of crossbows in China, the Battle of Crecy of the Hundred Years' War, which took place on August 26, 1346, first demonstrated the effectiveness of Edward III's English archers, composed mostly of newly recruited, socially shunned yeomen with longbows, against the respectable armored French knights of Philip VI.

Similarly, the Battle of Agincourt on October 25, 1415, decisively confirmed the obsolescence of hitherto invincible French aristocratic knights on horseback. In opposition, English yeomen, commoner foot-soldiers, members of a class unappreciated by their social betters in their home society, applied with glory in war a despised killing tool designed for illegal poaching in peace. Armed with a fresh military application of ignoble longbow technology, the socially inferior English yeomen in the form of simple unarmored infantry-archers, proved their battlefield supremacy to the socially superior French aristocrats in the form of powerfully armored mounted knights.

The Battle of Agincourt marked the end of the age of chivalry and announced the obsolescence of its stylized methods of warfare. It also heralded the beginning of a period in which the sovereign would look for military support from the gentry of his realm rather than traditionally from the aristocracy. This gave rise to the resulting political implication that henceforth war would have to be fought for national purpose or religious conviction rather than for settling private feuds among royalties.

In William Shakespeare's *Henry V,* the central scene of which features the Battle of Agincourt, the most glorious in English history, King Henry addresses his yeomen soldiers in a famous nationalistic exultation:

"Dishonor not your mothers; now attest
that those whom you call'd fathers did beget you.
Be copy now to men of grosser blood,
and teach them how to war. And you, good yeomen,
whose limbs were made in England, show us here the
mettle of your pasture; let us swear that you are worth
your breeding; which I doubt not; for there is none of you
so mean and base that hath not noble luster in your eyes.
I see you stand like greyhounds in the slips,
Straining upon the start. The game's afoot;
Follow your spirit; and, upon this charge
Cry 'God for Harry! England and Saint George!'"

After the battle scene, Shakespeare (1564-1616) has King Henry recount the French dead:

"The names of those their nobles that lie dead:
Charles Delabreth, High Constable of France;
The Master of the Cross-bows, Lord Rambures ..."

In ancient Chinese warfare, the code of honorable martial conduct required that combat be personal, bodily and frontal. Combatants were organized according to rank, as per all other social activities in a class-conscious and rigidly hierarchical society. *Jiangjun* (generals) were pitted against *jiangjun,* captains against captains and foot soldiers against foot soldiers. Social segregation was reflected in the proverb: "Earthenware does not deserve collision with porcelain."

Expertise in corporeal martial skill was so highly prized that *jiangjun* were frequently expected to engage personally in one-on-one combat with their opposing counterparts. Battles were sometimes won or lost depending on the outcome of high-ranking personal duels under the watchful eyes of troops on each side. By Tang time in the 7th century, however, the cult of martial chivalry in which individual valor determined the outcome of battles already had become only a legend of the past. Firepower was still considered cowardly. And the use of firearms was not acceptable to proud warriors as respectable members of the social elite. Until influenced in modern times by popular Hollywood films on the American Wild West, Chinese children playing war would prefer swordfights to gunfights.

Gunpowder remained unknown in the West until the late 10th century. However, Europeans abandoned outmoded rules of chivalry after the Middle Ages and enthusiastically incorporated firearms and artillery into the lexicon of their military arts after the late 15th century. In contrast, thanks to the Confucian aversion to technological progress, Chinese military planners did not modernize their martial code, basing foreign policy on the principle of civilized benevolence. They continued to suppress development of firearms as immoral and dishonorable up to the 19th century, much to China's misfortune.

As a result, European armies arrived in China in the 19th century with superior firearms. They consistently and repeatedly scored decisive victories with their small but better-armed expeditionary forces over the numerically superior yet technologically backward, sword-wielding Chinese army of the decrepit Qing Dynasty (1636-1911).

China's most influential revolutionary, Mao Zedong, proclaimed in modern times his famous dictum: "Political power comes from the barrel of a gun." He was in fact condemning the obsolete values of Confucianism *(ru jia)* as much as stating a truism in barbaric modern realpolitik.

Confucian ethics notwithstanding, morality and honor failed to save China from Western imperialism, because morality and honor require observation from both opponents. It was not a clash of civilizations, but a clash between civilization and barbarism. Militarism is a race toward barbarism camouflaged by technology as modernity.

The Boxers Uprising of 1900, the Chinese name for which is *Yihetuan* (Righteous Harmony Brigade), was an extremist xenophobic movement. It was encouraged as a chauvinistic instrument for domestic politics by the decrepit court of the Qing Dynasty, dominated by the self-indulging, reactionary Dowager Empress (Cixi Taihou, 1838-1908). **Notice the words "self-indulging and reactionary". Mr. Liu makes the point that these are the reasons behind the decrepit court of the Qing Dynasty.** The Boxer Uprising was used by the Dowager Empress as a populist counterweight to abort the budding "100 Days" elitist reform movement of 1898, led by conservative reformist Kang Youwei (1858-1927) around the young monarch, the weak Emperor Guangxu (reigned 1875-1908), belatedly and defensively advocating modernization for China.

The members of *Yihetuan,* in a burst of chauvinistic frenzy, rejected the use of modern and therefore foreign firearms in favor of traditional broadswords. They relied on protection against enemy bullets from Taoist amulets, their faith in which would remain unshaken in the face of undeniable empirical evidence provided by hundreds of thousands of falling comrades shot by Western gunfire. The term Boxer would be coined by bewildered Europeans whose modern pragmatism would fill them with a superficial superiority complex, justified on narrow grounds, over an ancient culture that stubbornly clung to the irrational power of faith, in defiance of reason. **Mr. Liu's statement is poignant; irrational**

29

faith exists in the physical but not the spiritual. He makes no distinction here so I want to make sure you get this.

Historians often trace the source of national predicaments to particular decisions made by leaders based on personal character, rather than to structural conditions of institutions. This convenient emphasis on personal political errors at the expense of deterministic institutional structure tends to nurture speculations that with wiser decisions, a socio-economic-political order trapped inside an obsolete institutional system would not necessarily be doomed to collapse under the strain of its own contradictions. Such speculations are hard to verify, since it can be argued that bad political decisions by faulty leaders are not independent of a nation's institutional defects. The penchant of the sole remaining superpower to resort to overwhelming force against those not willing to bend to its will may well be an institutional march from modernity back toward barbarism. **Now place this in a personal context; is our "need' to consume a matter of personal choice or are we trapped within an existing socio-economic system that decides for us?**

Ironically, the Boxers Uprising so discredited the public image of the stubbornly reactionary Qing court that, within a decade after its outbreak, the democratic revolution of Dr Sun Yat-sen succeeded in 1911 in overthrowing the three-century-old Qing Dynasty, despite the effective reactionary suppression of progressive monarchist reform efforts in the dynasty's last phase, or perhaps because of it. Extremist reactionaries, in their eagerness to be gravediggers for progressive reformers, usually become instead unwitting midwives for revolutionary radicals. The Taoist concept of the curative potential of even deadly poison was again demonstrated by the pathetic phenomenon of the Boxers Uprising.

Thus a case can be made that extreme fundamentalist opposition to the West may be the midwife for modernization of Islamic civilization. The capitalistic West nurtured and used Islamic fundamentalism as an antidote against communism in the oil regions of the Middle East during the Cold War, the same way it had nurtured and used fascism during the Great Depression. The antidote proves to be more lethal to the capitalistic West.

Western military prowess, with its arsenal of smart bombs and weapons of mass destruction ready for deployment to impose its will on others, is not a march toward modernity, but a retreat toward barbarism. A civilization built on militarization of the peace remains a barbaric civilization. What Western militarism has done is to abduct modernity as synonymous with Western civilization, depriving human civilization of an evolving process of cultural diversity. The effect of this abduction of modernity had been profound and comprehensive. **I can agree with Mr. Liu to a point but the fact remains that Islamic fundamentalism doesn't have subjugation of the West in mind; they want us dead. Liu conveniently overlooks this fact and assigns the word "barbarism" to the West's militaristic response. The West has no problem with cultural diversity; what a country and citizens do within their borders is their**

31

choice. What the West has a problem with is when a nation-entity decides that its way of life is better and chooses to impose its will on the West or any other nation-entity.

The West is not the only guilty party in history, only the most recent. Chinese civilization during the Qin Dynasty (221-207 BC) took a great step forward toward forging a unified nation and culture, but in the process lost much of the richness of its ancient, local traditions and rendered many details of its fragmented past incomprehensible to posterity. Universality and standardization, ingredients of progress, are mortal enemies of particularity and variety, components of tradition. Human civilization deserves a richer vision of modernity than that offered by the West. Until modernization is divorced from Westernization, non-Western civilizations will continue to resist modernization.

Tu Weiming, professor of Chinese history and philosophy and director of the Harvard-Yenching Institute at Harvard University, wrote: "Hegel, [Karl] Marx and Max Weber all shared the ethos that, despite all its shortcomings, the modern West informed by the Enlightenment mentality was the only arena where the true difference for the rest of the world could be made. Confucian East Asia, Islamic Middle East, Hindu India, or Buddhist Southeast Asia was on the receiving end of this process. Eventually, modernization as homogenization would make cultural diversity inoperative, if not totally meaningless. It was inconceivable that Confucianism or, for that matter, any other non-Western spiritual traditions could exert a

32

shaping influence on the modernizing process. The development from tradition to modernity was irreversible and inevitable."

Tu suggests that, in the global context, what some of the most brilliant minds in the modern West assumed to be self-evidently true turned out to be parochial. In the rest of the world and, arguably, in Western Europe and North America, the anticipated clear transition from tradition to modernity never occurred. As a norm, traditions continue to make their presence in modernity and, indeed, the modernizing process itself is constantly shaped by a variety of cultural forms rooted in distinct traditions. The recognition of the relevance of radical otherness to one's own self-understanding of the 18th century seems more applicable to the current situation in the global community than the inattention to any challenges to the modern Western mindset of the 19th century and the first half of the 20th. For example, the outstanding Enlightenment thinkers such as Francois Arouet de Voltaire, Gottfried Leibniz and Jean Jacques Rousseau took China as their major reference society and Confucianism as their major reference culture. It seems that toward the 21st century, the openness of the 18th century, as contrasted with the exclusivity of the 19th century, may provide a better guide for the dialogue of civilizations.

According to Professor Tu, in light of the ill-conceived hypothesis of the "coming clash of civilizations, the need for civilizational dialogues and for exploring a global ethic is more compelling. Among the Enlightenment values advocated by the French Revolution, fraternity, the functional equivalent of community, has received scant attention among modern political theorists. The preoccupation with fixing the relationship between the individual and the state since [John] Locke's treatises on government is, of course, not the full picture of modern political thought; but it is undeniable that communities, notably the family, have been ignored as irrelevant in the mainstream of Western political discourse."

In Tu's view, East Asian modernity under the influence of Confucian traditions suggests an alternative model to Western modernism:

(1) Government leadership in a market economy is not only necessary but is also desirable. The doctrine that government is a necessary evil and that the market in itself can provide an "invisible hand" for ordering society is antithetical to modern experience in either the West or the East. A government that is responsive to public needs, responsible for the welfare of the people and accountable to society at large is vitally important for the creation and maintenance of order.

(2) Although law is essential as the minimum requirement for social stability, "organic solidarity" can only result from the implementation of humane rites of interaction. The civilized mode of conduct can never be communicated through coercion. Exemplary teaching as a standard of inspiration invites voluntary participation. Law alone cannot generate a sense of shame to guide civilized behavior. It is the ritual act that encourages people to live up to their own aspirations.

34

(3) Family as the basic unit of society is the locus from which the core values are transmitted. The dyadic relationships within the family, differentiated by age, gender, authority, status, and hierarchy, provide a richly textured natural environment for learning the proper way of being human. The principle of reciprocity, as a two-way traffic of human interaction, defines all forms of human-relatedness in the family. Age and gender, potentially two of the most serious gaps in the primordial environment of the human habitat, are brought into a continuous flow of intimate sentiments of human care.

(4) Civil society flourishes not because it is an autonomous arena above the family and beyond the state. Its inner strength lies in its dynamic interplay between family and state. The image of the family as a microcosm of the state and the ideal of the state as an enlargement of the family indicate that family stability is vitally important for the body politic and a vitally important function of the state is to ensure organic solidarity of the family. Civil society provides a variety of mediating cultural institutions that allow for a fruitful articulation between family and state. The dynamic interplay between the private and public enables the civil society to offer diverse and enriching resources for human flourishing.

(5) Education ought to be the civil religion of society. The primary purpose of education is character-building. Intent on the cultivation of the full person, schools should emphasize ethical as well as cognitive intelligence. Schools should teach the art of accumulating "social capital" through communication. In addition to the acquisition of knowledge and skills, schooling must be

congenial to the development of cultural competence and appreciation of spiritual values.

(6) Since self-cultivation is the root for the regulation of family, governance of state, and peace under heaven, the quality of life of a particular society depends on the level of self-cultivation of its members. A society that encourages self-cultivation as a necessary condition for human flourishing is a society that cherishes virtue-centered political leadership, mutual exhortation as a communal way of self-realization, the value of the family as the proper home for learning to be human, civility as the normal pattern of human interaction and, education as character-building.

Tu acknowledges that it is far-fetched to suggest that these societal ideals are fully realized in East Asia. Actually, East Asian societies often exhibit behaviors and attitudes just the opposite of the supposed salient features of Confucian modernity indicate. Indeed, having been humiliated by imperialism and colonialism for decades, the rise of East Asia, on the surface at least, blatantly displays some of the most negative aspects of Western modernism with a vengeance: exploitation, mercantilism, consumerism, materialism, greed, egoism and brutal competitiveness.

Nevertheless, as the first non-Western region to become modernized, the cultural implications of the rise of "Confucian" East Asia are far-reaching. The modern West as informed by the Enlightenment mentality provided the initial impetus for worldwide social transformation. The historical reasons that prompted the modernizing process in Western Europe and North America are not necessarily structural components of modernity. Surely, Enlightenment values such as instrumental rationality, liberty, rights consciousness, due process of law, privacy and individualism are all universalizable modern values. However, as the Confucian example suggests, "Asian values" such as sympathy, distributive justice, duty-consciousness, ritual, public-spiritedness and group orientation are also universalizable modern values. Just as the former ought to be incorporated into East Asian modernity, the latter may turn out to be a critical and timely reference for the American way of life.

Chapter 3 - THE ABDUCTION OF MODERNITY Part 2: That Old Time Religion

From the fall of the Roman Empire to the 15th century, Islam was the dominant civilization outside of China. The Islamic world of this period was more advanced, with greater wealth and a higher level of culture than the Christian West. Islamic scholars preserved the texts of the ancient Greek philosophers and scientists by translating them into Arabic and Latin, which Renaissance scholars emerging from the Dark Ages relied on for sources and scholarship on antiquity. Arabs made path-breaking advances in mathematics, astronomy, medicine and philosophy, and transmitted to the West much of what they had learned from China. The West through the interpretation of Arab eyes rediscovered much of Western antiquity.

Mohammed the Prophet entered Mecca in AD 630 and established Islamic rule. The growing forces of Muslim, 121 years from that date, after having conquered Spain, North Africa, Egypt, Persia and much of Byzantium, decisively defeated the Tang Chinese army in 751 at the famous Battle of Talas, between modern-day Tashkent and Lake Balkhash. The Arab victory was aided by a branch of Muslim Tujue (Turkic) tribes known as Karluks, who launched a surprised attack on Tang forces from the rear. The Battle of Talas halted Chinese expansion into Central Asia.

The Chinese refer to Arabs as *Dashi,* from the Syrian word *Tayi* or the Persian word *T'cyk.* The Arabs conquered Samarkand in the 8th century. For five centuries thereafter, Samarkand flourished under the Omayyad Arabs as a trade center between Baghdad and Changan, the capital of dynastic China, until advances in sea transport in the 13th century finally rendered the Silk Route economically obsolete. Chinese prisoners captured by Arab forces at the Battle of Talas in 751 eventually introduced the art of paper-making to Arab lands and subsequently to Europe, but only after Arab paper-makers, jealously guarding the secret from Europeans for five more centuries, had sold paper to Europe at handsome profits in the interim. A process to make paper from vegetable fiber had first been invented by Cailun in China during the Han Dynasty in 105. The first paper mill outside of China was established by Arabs in Samarkand six-and-a-half centuries later in 751. The invention of paper greatly facilitated the development of language, graphic arts and culture, first in China, then in the Arab world, and then in the West.

The scientific and industrial revolutions vastly increased the wealth and power of the West from the middle of the 19th century. After the defeat of the Islamic Ottoman

Empire in World War I, the Middle East was taken over by European powers and broken up into colonies and protectorates. Today, despite decolonization, nationalism and oil riches, this region remains poor and underdeveloped, not because modernity bypassed it, but because modernity arrived in the form of neo-colonialism. Westernization in these lands has produced miserable results, forcing the Islamic world to the conclusion that the solution may be a renewal of the Islamic faith that reigned in the days of their former greatness. The West derides this view as a rejection of modernity, notwithstanding historical evidence of the Arab world having embraced science and technology at a time when the best minds in the West were still prisoners of the flat-Earth doctrine. **Liu is correct in his iteration of history but blames Western culture to the downfall of the Islamic Empire. He fails to point out that Islam pressed its culture on all conquered people's at the tip of a sword and many so-called "Arab inventions" cited were stolen from conquered peoples. This notwithstanding, he is correct in his citing the scientific and industrial revolutions as the causes behind Western wealth and the beginning of massive consumption.**

The clash-of-civilizations theme exaggerates unity in outlook, values, ideas, and loyalties among people who share the common history and culture that define a civilization. Modern wars have been fought mostly within Western civilization, while easy imperialistic conquests have been the order of the day between Western and non-Western civilizations. Samuel P Huntington wrote: "The central characteristics of the West, those which distinguish it from other civilizations, antedate the modernization of the West." Thus the modernization of other civilizations is not in conflict with rejection of Westernization. The scholar Bernard Lewis, in seeing hatred of modernity as the main driving force in the wider context of Islamic terrorism, is confusing modernity with Western culture.

The rejection of modernity occurs in every nation and civilization. The history of the West, dominated by the rise of Christianity, is strewn with wars of resistance against modernity. The history of Christianity, the main thread of Western history, is a continuing saga against modernity. The US "war on terrorism" itself is a continuation of this resistance in its emphasis on force rather than understanding. **This is one statement that is pure garbage. Numerous attempts at diplomacy and understanding have failed. Why? There is big money in terrorism and evil in general. The Somali pirates are prime examples. Islamic fundamentalism hides behind religion when all they want is to own the world and all of its wealth.** By abducting the concept of modernity as a monopoly of the West, Western scholars obstruct true modernity in a diverse world. Modernity is defined by the West as a collection of Western values arbitrarily deemed universal - the secular culture of circular rationality, materialist science, alienating individualism, technical innovation, amoral legalism, selective democracy and exploitative capitalism that Western imperialism has spread worldwide in different forms and to varying degrees. Religious fundamentalism is currently enjoying unprecedented influence over secular politics within the United States, as exemplified

41

by President George W Bush's proclamation that God, not the US constitution, told him to attack Afghanistan and Iraq. While the separation of church and state is still a governing tenet in the US, separation of religion and politics is non-existent.

Modernity, a new version of Rudyard Kipling's "white man's burden" of old-fashioned imperialism, has been brought to the world by neo-imperialism, to disarm resistance to Western neo-imperialist encroachment. Opposition to exploitative policies and actions of the imperialist West is dismissed as irrational hatred of modernity. Kipling (1865-1936) confused Western materialist advancement with moral superiority, as measured by a standard based on virtue. Kipling's romantic portrayal of the model Englishman as brave, honorable, conscientious and self-reliant, while popularly accepted in the English-speaking West, would be generally rejected in the East by those with direct exposure to the breed as being still unwashed of animalistic instincts. The idealized image would be recognized as being a wishful manifestation based on Kipling's apologetic colonial mentality toward his social betters in his home society. It is also a compensation for Kipling's own inferiority complex derived from his love-hate relationship with the richness of Indian culture, to which he was attracted but which he was unable to appreciate fully because of his deep-rooted racial prejudice as a product of Western culture.

The "white man's burden" is a worldview for justifying imperialism. The term is the name of an 1899 poem by Kipling, the sentiments of which give insight into this worldview.

The first verse of the Kipling poem reads:

Take up the White Man's burden -
Send forth the best ye breed -
Go, bind your sons to exile
To serve your captives' need;
To wait, in heavy harness,
On fluttered folk and wild -
Your new-caught sullen peoples,
Half devil and half child.

In this view, non-European cultures are seen as childlike and devilish, with people of European descent having a sacred and selfless obligation to dominate them in perpetuity for their own good and salvation.

The poem was originally published in a popular US magazine (McClure's). It was written specifically to address US isolationist sentiments after the Spanish-American War in 1898, from which the United States would emerge as a world power of consequence. Kipling wrote this poem specifically to help sway popular opinion in the US, so that a "friendly" Western power would hold the strategically important Philippines after the collapse of the Spanish empire in Southeast Asia.

The view and the term by now are widely regarded as racist. Nevertheless, it served the purpose of allowing colonization to proceed in the context of US anti-colonialism self-image and to legitimize historical racism in the United States.

The colonial powers relied on the excuse of "civilizing" indigenous peoples to rationalize colonialism. Archeological findings in South Africa were suppressed for fear that the existence of sophisticated urban culture in southern Africa prior to European colonization would pose a threat to the argument that white rule was necessary to "civilize" the region.

The term "white man's burden" is sometimes used in the present time to describe double standards toward those of European descent because of perceived responsibility or culpability for historical wrongs. It is the main moral argument for affirmative action in the United States. Increasingly vocal demands are heard from the black community and the nations of indigenous people in the US for an official apology and a program of restitution to address such historical wrongs perpetrated by one people on others.

Cultural imperialism is the practice of promoting the culture and language of one national civilization in another for the purpose of political and social control. This can take the form of active, formal policy, such as in education and job opportunities, or a general attitude of superiority complex.

Empires throughout history have been established using war and physical compulsion. In the long term, the invading population tended to become absorbed into the dominant local culture, or acquire its attributes indirectly. Cultural imperialism reverses this trend by imposing an alien culture on the conquered. One of the early examples of cultural imperialism was the extinction of the Etruscan culture and language caused by the imperial policies of the Romans.

The Greek culture built gymnasiums, theaters and public baths in places that its adherents conquered, such as ancient Judea, where Greek cultural imperialism sparked a popular revolt, with the effect that the subject populations became immersed in the conquering culture. The spread of the *koine* (common) Greek language was another large factor in this immersion.

The prayer-book rebellion of 1549, when the English state sought to suppress non-English languages with the English-language *Book of Common Prayer,* is another example. In replacing Latin with English, and under the guise of suppressing Catholicism, English was in effect imposed as the language of the Anglican Church as a dominant societal institution. Though people in many areas of Cornwall did not speak or understand English at the time, the Cornish language fell into disuse as a result. The Cornish people protested against the imposition of an English prayer book, resulting in large numbers of protesters being massacred by the king's army, their leaders executed and the people suffering harsh reprisals.

Throughout the 18th and 19th centuries the dominant English establishment attempted to eliminate all non-English languages within the British Isles (such as Welsh, Irish and Scottish Gaelic) by outlawing them or otherwise marginalizing their speakers. Many other languages had almost or totally been wiped out, including Cornish and Manx. "Cultural imperialism" is a term first applied to the

British Empire, with its many measures to impose the conquering culture on the conquered. These ranged from pound-sterling hegemony, to the preferred social status given the game of cricket and English dress codes, to mandatory use and teaching of English, further to establish Britain's control on nations and territories within the empire. Language imperialism is the basic element in cultural imperialism. The discriminatory practice of proper elocution is a component of in-group cultural imperialism.

As exploration of the Americas increased, European nations including Britain, France, Belgium, the Netherlands, Spain and Portugal all raced to claim territory in hopes of generating increased economic wealth for themselves. In these new colonies, the European conquerors imposed their languages and cultures on lands whose indigenous population was too large or too established to annihilate. The same took place in Africa and Asia. The record of US policy and abuse of Native Americans is atrocious, going beyond cultural imperialism to genocide.

During the late 18th, the 19th and the early 20th centuries, the Swedish government continually repressed the Saami culture. Repression took numerous forms, such as banning the Saami language and by forceful removal of many cultural artifacts, such as the magic drums of the *naajds* (Saami shamans). Most of the drums have not to date been returned. Even as late as the 1960s the Sweden-Finnish people of the Torne Valley had their native Finnish dialect banned from use in schools and public records.

Cultural imperialism since World War II has primarily been connected with the US. Most countries outside the United States view the pervasive US cultural export through business and popular culture as threatening to their traditional ways of life or moral values. Some countries, including France and Canada, have adopted official policies that actively oppose "Americanization". Representatives of al-Qaeda stated that their attacks on US interests were motivated in part by a reaction to perceived US cultural imperialism.

Edward Said of Columbia University, one of the pioneers of post-colonial studies, has written extensively on the subject of cultural imperialism. His work highlights the misconceived assumptions about cultures and societies and is influenced by Michel Foucault's concepts of discourse and power. Foucault views the intellectual's role as no longer to place himself somewhat ahead and to the side in order to express the stifled truth of the collectivity. Rather, it is to struggle against the forms of power that transform him into its object and instrument in the sphere of knowledge, truth, consciousness, and discourse. In this sense theory does not express, translate, or serve to apply practice: it *is* practice. But it is local and regional and not totalizing. This is a struggle against power, a struggle aimed at revealing and undermining power where it is most invisible and insidious. It is not to awaken consciousness that we struggle but to sap power, to take power; it is an activity conducted alongside those who struggle for power, and not their illumination. Colonialism, the political theory governing imperialism, is based on a belief that the mores of the colonizer are superior to those of the colonized on the basis on power. This colonial mentality explains why former colonies such as Hong Kong cling to the myth of the superiority of their colonial culture.

According to Said, the Orient signifies a system of representations framed by political forces that brought the Orient into Western learning, Western consciousness, and Western Empire. The Orient exists for the West, and is constructed by and in relation to the West. Orientalism refers to the study of Near and Far Eastern societies and cultures, generally by Westerners. It is a mirror image of what are inferior and alien ("Other") to the West. Although this term had been abandoned as archaic by the late 20th century, Said argues that the term should be redefined to apply to any current study of such societies to correct current accounts of the Middle East, India, China, and elsewhere that reflects long-held Western biases. The discourse and visual imagery of Orientalism are laced with notions of power and superiority, formulated initially to facilitate a colonizing mission on the part of the West and perpetuated through a wide variety of discourses and policies.

Critical theorists regard Orientalism as part of an effort to justify colonialism through the concept of the "white man's burden", and to wield the sword of modernity against allegedly "backward" civilizations. A critical theory is an account of morality that is sensitive to the historically contingent nature of the culture that spawned it: by adopting a hypothetical stance toward their own traditions and on this basis grasping their own cultural relativity, participants in the formation of a critical theory take a questioning stance toward their own practices while nonetheless avoiding the paralysis of moral relativism. The current coercive application of the Western concept of democracy, rule of law, individual freedom and market fundamentalism as universal truth is a legitimate target of critical theory.

Promoters of this Western version of modernity see its birth in the West through a radical transformation of its past. The West of the Middle Ages, built around a worldview of Christian Scholasticism, was a society of religious philosophy, feudal law, and an agricultural economy. Out of this past, the Renaissance and Enlightenment produced a substantially new mentality of science, individualism, industrial capitalism and imperialism. The cultural foundation of this new mentality is that reason, not revelation, is the instrument of knowledge and arbiter of truth; that science, not religion, leads to truth about nature and life; that the pursuit of happiness in this life, not the quest for spiritual fulfillment, or suffering in preparation for the next, is the cardinal purpose of existence; that reason can and should be used to increase human control through economic and technological progress; that the individual person is an end in him/herself with the capacity to direct his/her own life, not a communal member of society with a prescribed social role; that individuals should be encouraged to indulge in inalienable rights to freedom of thought, speech, and action; that religious belief should be a private affair rather than a collective awareness, that intolerance is a social disease, and that church and state should be kept separate.

As the West grows stronger, tolerance of other cultures and of those within the West itself who refuse to participate is viewed increasingly as a sign of weakness. Domination takes on sophisticated, less visible forms. National sovereignty is pushed aside in the name of replacing command economies with markets, warfare with trade, and rule by king or commissar with token democracy. To resist neo-imperialism is to resist modernity. This view justifies the new empire of the sole superpower, self-proclaimed inheritor of Western civilization.

Yet this view of modernity misreads history. Thomas Aquinas (1225-71) benefited intellectually from his exposure to translations of works of Aristotle from Greek into Latin by Arab scholars to whose worldview he became much indebted. He also profited intellectually from the rise of universities in Europe during 12th and 13th centuries, notably the University of Bologna (1088), known for its studies in law, the University of Padua (founded by dissidents from Bologna), the University of Paris, and Oxford University, all founded as centers of learning in theology, not science. In this new intellectual milieu in Europe, Aquinas applied Aristotelian syllogism as interpreted by Arab minds to medieval mysticism of revelation. His *Summa Theologica* (1267-73) was a systematic exposition of theology on rational philosophical principles worked out by the ancient Greeks as modified by Arab precision and algebra, which pioneered the use of variables in problem-solving in logic.

Up to that time, while Scholasticism, as advanced by St Augustine (354-430), would vindicate reason in theology, it would carefully differentiate between theology and philosophy. It would do so by confining theology, proceeding from faith, to investigations of revealed truths, while it would limit philosophy, based on reason, from concern with truths that transcended reason. Revealed truth would be proclaimed as discoverable only through faith.

The 13th century was a critical point in Christian thought regarding the relationship between faith and reason. The intellectual community in Christendom at that time was torn between claims of followers of Averroes (1126-98), Arabian philosopher from Cordoba in Spain, and claims of followers of St Augustine, troubled youth turned zealous convert, founder of Christian theology and spokesman for Christian mysticism.

Efforts of followers of Averroes in the 13th century to separate absolutely faith from truth clashed with the traditional claim of truth being exclusively a matter of faith. Such a claim had been made for the past nine centuries by followers of St Augustine, whose contribution to the evolution of Christianity was considered second only to that of St Paul, apostle to Gentiles and the greatest missionary apostle. Paul laid down the relentless approach of Western evangelism by applying to his missionary zeal the same vigor and intolerance he showed toward the persecution of Christians before his epiphany on the road to Damascus.

Averroes, Latin name for Abu-al-Walid Ibn Rushd, whose commentaries on Aristotle would remain influential for four centuries until the Renaissance, attempted to circumscribe the separate limits of faith and reason. He asserted that both could process truths and that the two separate realms need not be reconciled because they are not in conflict. Siger de Brabant of the University of Paris, leader of the Averroists, claimed in 1260 that it should be possible, as a matter of veracity, and tolerable, as a license in intellectual soundness, for a concept to be true in reason but false in faith or vice versa.

The doctrines of the Averroists, which include denying the immortality of the individual soul and upholding the eternity of matter, ended up being officially condemned by the Catholic Church.

St Thomas Aquinas, nicknamed Dumb Ox because of his slow and deliberate manner of speech, brilliant father of Neo-Scholasticism, aiming to resolve the dispute between Averroists and Augustinians, would hold that reason and faith constitute two harmonious realms in which the truth of faith complements that of reason, both being gifts of God, but reason having an autonomy of its own. The existence of God could therefore be discovered through reason, with the grace of God.

The theological significance of this momentous claim by Thomas Aquinas cannot be over-emphasized. It would save Christianity from falling into irrelevance in the Age of Reason, sometimes referred to as the Enlightenment, and preserve tolerance for faith among rational thinkers in the scientific world. The Thomist claim remained unchallenged for five centuries until David Hume (1711-86) pointed out in his *Inquiry into Human Understanding* that since the conclusion of a valid inference could contain no information not found in the premise, there could be no valid conclusion from observed to unobserved phenomena.

Hume let the logic air out of the Thomist natural-theology balloon, and in the process showed that even general laws of science could not be logically justified beyond their own limits, perhaps even including his own sweeping conclusion. Hume, the empiricist, would logically determine that logic is circular and goes nowhere: a classic position of Taoist skepticism.

Immanuel Kant (1724-1804) emancipated man's command of knowledge from Humean skepticism. In his *Critique of Pure Reason* (1781), Kant emphasized the contribution of the knower to knowledge. While acknowledging that the three great issues of metaphysics - God, freedom and immortality - could not be logically determined, he asserted that their essence is a necessary presupposition. In his subsequent publications, *Critique of Practical Reason* (1788) and *Critique of Judgement* (1790), Kant asserted as a moral law his famous categorical imperative requiring moral actions to be unconditionally and universally binding to absolute goodwill. Goodwill is singularly absent in imperialism, classic or neo.

Notwithstanding the enlightened breakthroughs of English Protestant empiricists such as Thomas Hobbes,

John Locke and David Hume, and perhaps in reaction to them, Pope Leo XIII issued the encyclical *Aeterni Patris* in 1879. It declared Scholasticism, as modified by Thomas Aquinas, to be official Catholic philosophy. Unwittingly, Scholasticism legitimized the independence of secular politics from Church control. If reason and faith constitute two harmonious realms in which the truth of faith complements that of reason, both being gifts of God, but reason having an autonomy of its own, then politics and religion can also belong to separate realms in which morality of religion complements virtue in politics, but politics having an autonomy of its own. It provided the theological rationalization for the separation of church and state.

Thus when Sayyid Qutb (1906-66), leader of the Muslim Brotherhood in Egypt and prolific author of great influence, wrote: "An all-out offensive, a jihad, should be waged against modernity so that ... moral rearmament could take place. The ultimate objective is to re-establish the Kingdom of Allah upon earth," he was rejecting not modernity but the modernity of the West. Qutb was not preaching for suffering in preparation for the next life as Western scholars such as Bernard Lewis allege, he wanted his civilization back and he wanted it now. **Again, Liu fails to see the economics behind Arab "jihad" insofar as jihad pays well and terrorists of all kinds wage cowardly war for material gains first while hiding behind some credo or belief.**

Qutb did not write out of ignorance of the West. His fundamentalism was formed during the two years he spent in the United States, which seemed to him "a disastrous combination of avid materialism and egoistic individualism". Alexis de Tocqueville (1805-59), while admiring the energy and versatility of Americans, also thought they were too intent on making money and would be condemned to a commercial culture. In Tocqueville's opinion, Americans' notion of equality was derived from their "general equality of condition" rather than from moral commitment and that their equality might eventually be endangered by the domination of a new industrial class. Mawlana Abu'l-A'la Mawdudi (1903-79), the founder of the fundamentalist Jama'at-i Islami in India and Pakistan, was also militantly opposed to individualism. In an Islamic state, he wrote, "no one can regard any field of his affairs as personal and private". **True, this paragraph blatantly describes capitalism; removing individualism removes innovation and prosperity, both of which everyone enjoys while the expound against it.**

Modern Asia cannot be fully understood without a thorough awareness of Confucianism, Buddhism and Taoism. Western influence, from Christianity to liberalism to Marxism, has only been an ill-fitted costume over an ancient culture deeply rooted in Confucian values, Buddhist enlightenment mercy and Taoist paradox. Feudal culture in China has aspects of what modern political science would label fascist, socialist, democratic and anarchist. As a socio-political system, feudalism is inherently authoritarian and totalitarian. However, since feudal cultural ideals have always been meticulously nurtured by Confucianism to be congruent with the political regime, social control, while pervasive, is seldom consciously felt as oppression by the general public. Or, more accurately, social oppression - both vertical, such as sovereign to subject, and horizontal, such as gender prejudice - is considered natural for lack of an accepted alternative vision. Concepts such as equality, individuality, privacy, personal freedom and democracy are deemed antisocial, and only longed for by the deranged-of-mind, such as radical Taoists. This was true in large measure up to modern times when radical Taoists were transformed into radical political and cultural dissidents. **Liu speaks eloquently against the West's intolerance to eastern traditions but fails to see the intolerance of the eastern socio-economic model as being intolerant to everyone including their own peoples.**

Buddhism *(Fo Jiao)* first appeared in China officially in AD 65. Some evidence suggests that it might have been imported to China from India as early as 2 BC. Since its introduction, Buddhism has permeated Chinese society and its economic life, despite periodic suppression by the state. It had affected the customs of all levels of society by the time of the Tang Dynasty some six centuries after its introduction. Buddhist temples, monasteries and shrines had been established in every part of the empire. The services of *sengs* (Buddhist monks) became indispensable for all social events, performing religious ceremonies for funerals and weddings, blessings for newborns, administering temples for the faithful and attending family shrines for the elite. *Sengs* functioned as preachers, teachers, scribes, artists and even doctors. Often they would become top advisors to the *huangdi* (emperor), and many *sengs* would even become powerful political figures both at court and at the local level.

The name Buddha *(Fo)* is a Sanskrit word meaning Enlightened One. It is the appellation conferred by the faithful on Indian Prince Siddhartha Gautama (563-483 BC), who came from the southern foothills of the Himalayas.

Buddhism originated at the end of 5th century BC in the valley of the middle Ganges in India. The religious sect first rose as a plebeian reaction to claims of spiritual and social supremacy by Hindu Brahman priests who were the ruling elite of the Indian caste system. Since that time, Buddhism has spread across political, social and ethnic boundaries as one of the three great religions of the world, the other two being Christianity and Islam.

Curiously, acceptance of Buddhism remained sporadic in India, its birthplace. The incorporation of Buddha by Hinduism as the ninth incarnation (avatar) of its god, Vishnu, seriously adulterated the autonomous uniqueness of Buddhism in India. The Muslim invasion of India from the 11th century gradually but effectively obliterated remaining Buddhist communities there. Similarly, Christianity remains a minority religion in the Middle East, its holy place of origin.

Kanishka, an ardent patron of Buddhism, was king of the Kushan Empire, which dominated northern India during the 2nd century AD. He was also known in history as the sponsor of a Greco-Buddhist style of sculpture, labeled by art historians as the Gandhara School, typified by curly-haired seated Buddha statues, which became the dominant Buddhist art form in East Asia. A gilded bronze

Buddha of the Gandhara School is on display at the Harvard Fogg Art Museum in Cambridge, Massachusetts. More significant, Kanishka was instrumental in introducing Buddhism into Central Asia, whence it spread first to China, then Korea and finally Japan.

The branch of Buddhism that diffused into East Asia would take on different characteristics from the early sects of Buddha's own time. It would come to be known as Mahayana (*Dasheng,* meaning major vehicle), the scripture of which is written in classical Sanskrit, distinguishing itself from the older Hinayana (*Xiaosheng,* meaning minor vehicle), the scripture of which is written in a vernacular dialect (Prakrit) known as Pali. Hinayana Buddhism, remaining closer to ancient Buddhism, is practiced widely in Southeast Asia today.

The Sermon of the Turning of the Wheel of the Law, delivered by Buddha at Sarnath around 500 BC, elucidates the secret of a happy life by means of the Four Exalted Truths:

Truth I: Existence encompasses sorrow.

Truth II: Sorrow emanates from desire.
Truth III: Sorrow subsides when desire wanes.
Truth IV: Desire can be alleviated by following the Gracious Eight-Spectrum Path.

This Gracious Eight-Spectrum Path consists of:
Spectrum

1: Virtuous conviction. Spectrum

2: Virtuous resolution: to renounce sensual pleasure, to harm no living creatures and ultimately to achieve salvation.
Spectrum
3: Virtuous speech. Spectrum
4: Virtuous conduct. Spectrum
5: Virtuous involvement. Spectrum
6: Virtuous effort: to keep the mind free from evil and devoted to good. Spectrum
7: Virtuous contemplation. Spectrum
8: Virtuous meditation: to achieve an awareness of internal selflessness and external detachment.

Buddhist concerns are more ethical than metaphysical, focusing on human suffering, which is considered as inherent in life itself. Suffering can be dispelled only by abandoning desires such as ambition, selfishness, envy and greed. This approach to life is the diametrical opposite of the Western concept of modernity.

Detachment is key. Buddhists take vows against killing, stealing, falsehood, unchasteness and intoxication. They practice self-confession and try to live austere, ascetic lives with the objective of achieving nirvana, a state of blissful detachment that, when attained permanently, known as pari-nirvana, brings an end to the otherwise never-ending cycle of earth-bound rebirths through transmigration of the soul. The Four Exalted Truths of Buddhism have helped devotees deal with the tribulations of life. The Third Exalted Truth, sorrow subsides when desire wanes, has application to modern market economy. A basic Buddhist tenet: the secret of happiness is not getting what you want, but wanting what you get. So much for the concept of the pursuit of happiness in Western modernity. For the Buddhist idea of happiness, if you have to pursue it, you have lost it.

The reasons for China's popular embrace of Buddhism are complex and have been subject to constant reassessment. One commonly acknowledged reason is that Buddhism, while of foreign origin, shares commonality with both Taoist and Confucian concepts that are indigenous to Chinese culture. The passive side of Buddhism is Taoism, which practices contemplation and promotes self-awareness. And the active side of Buddhism is Confucianism, which advocates respect for authority and submission to propriety. Furthermore, Buddhism has provided, as it has evolved in China, elaborate, colorful ceremonies welcomed by one aspect of the collective Chinese character, hitherto suppressed through centuries of Confucian social restraint and Taoist self-denial.

Most of all, Buddhism fills a void left by traditional ancient Chinese religious concepts, which are centered rigidly around the trinity: 1) Heaven (Tian) - God. 2) Son of Heaven (Tianzi) - Emperor (sovereign). 3) The Hundred Surnames *(Baixing)* - People.

Heaven (Tian) is the abstract symbol of all things supernatural and authoritative, much like the manner in which the imperial court is referred to as the authoritative and decision-making body of the secular empire. God, a term that has no exact equivalent in the language of polytheistic Chinese culture, has its closest translation as Tiandi (King in Heaven), who is the highest god. Heaven as a realm is believed to be inhabited by a clan of gods and spirits *(shen-gui),* with hierarchical ranks, headed by Tiandi, similar to the Greek hierarchical community of gods headed by Zeus.

The secular *huangdi* (emperor) is the Son of Heaven (Tianzi), and the people, known as the Hundred Surnames *(Baixing),* are wards of *huangdi.* The people do not enjoy the privilege of directly communicating with Heaven, the domain of gods headed by Tiandi. The people's duty is to pay homage to the Son of Heaven, who alone possesses the privilege of communicating with and thanksgiving to Heaven. The most solemn ritual in Chinese feudal culture is the *fengshan* rites. It is a ritual that confers Heaven's abdication of authority on secular affairs in favor of *huangdi.*

Thus religion in China, before the arrival of Buddhism, had merely been a spiritual subsystem of the secular world. It was a spiritual extension of the rigid hierarchy of the ancient Chinese socio-political realm. Buddhism provided a previously unavailable outlet of direct religious expression for the common people. It introduced participatory religious experience into Chinese society. Whereas, in the context of the rigid Confucian social structure, Taoism *(Dao Jia)* provides the Chinese people with introverted individual spiritual freedom, Buddhism provides them with extroverted collective spiritual liberation, independent of communal hierarchy. Taoism allows the individual to contemplate privately, freeing him from the mental tyranny of an all-controlling culture, while Buddhism allows the people to worship independently, freeing them from the pervasive control of a rigid secular socio-political hierarchy.

Religion in China has a different meaning than in the West. The term "religion" in the Chinese language is composed of two characters: *zong-jiao,* literally meaning "ancestral teaching". Until the spread of Buddhism, religious experience for the Chinese people had been limited to reverence toward the spirits of their departed ancestors. Buddhism provided the average devotee with direct access to God without requiring a denial of reverence for ancestral spirits. Until the introduction of Christianity, the Chinese were not required by religion to deny the spirituality of their ancestors. This demand for the rejection of ancestor worship was a key obstacle preventing Christianity from becoming a major religion in China. Incidentally, even in Christian theology, "God" is translated in Chinese as Shangdi, meaning "The King Above". It is a celestial echo of the supreme ruler in the secular political system.

From its beginning, Buddhism took on an anti-establishment posture, which it moderated as it developed in China but never totally abandoned. Traditionally, in the early part of an emperor's reign, as soon as his rule was firmly established, he would perform the elaborate and formal *fengshan* rites. These Confucian rites of theocratic feudalism involve the paying of tribute by Tianzi (Son of Heaven) as *huangdi* (emperor), on behalf of his *baixing,* namely the people, to Tian (Heaven) where the head god Tiandi (King in Heaven) reigns. Through the *fengshan* rites, the *huangdi* received tribute and accepted loyalty pledges from his vassal lords on behalf of their many minions and subjects throughout the empire. Anyone besides the *huangdi* performing religious rites directly to Heaven would be committing forbidden acts tantamount to treasonous usurpation. Buddhism broke the monopolistic hold of the *huangdi* on religious celebration and opened it to all for the taking. Little wonder Buddhism spread like wildflowers.

By breaking down the hierarchical religious monopoly implied by Confucian *fengshan* rites, Buddhism in its early history in China unwittingly contributed to the crumbling of the foundation of a feudal hierarchy already in decline. Buddhism's populist theology bolstered the emergence of a secular structure in the form of a centrally managed empire, replacing autonomous local authority. In this new secular structure individuals could participate more freely in social functions, unrestricted by traditional local hierarchy.

The Buddhist notion of nirvana runs parallel to the concept of the Mandate of Heaven (Tianming). Ironically, by claiming that a state of nirvana could be earned through religious devotion by any deserving member of society, it implies that the Mandate of Heaven can also be earned by any deserving hero. Thus Buddhism invited periodic and recurring suppression from paranoid emperors who felt obliged to adopt anti-subversive measures against Buddhism, in order to defend the imperial claim on the Mandate of Heaven from challenges by ambitious members of the aristocracy who were Buddhist devotees.

While Buddhism serves as the fountainhead of the idea of open access for all to spiritual salvation, such universal access is dependent on the grace of detachment as exemplified by Buddha. This idea is akin to the detached central authority in an empire structure with the grace of a distant emperor who is less involved with the details of daily living of his subjects. It is less akin to the archaic hierarchical feudalism of autonomous local lords who control every detail of the lives of his fief. Thus Buddhism facilitated its own growth at the same time that it provided the philosophical justification for the flowering of a distant centralized political order in a complex, multi-dimensional society. The development of such a benign centralized political structure, first budding in imperial China in the 5th century, gathered unstoppable momentum around the 7th century.

The Buddhist concept of universal open access to nirvana had socio-political implications. It helped shift politics from being a contest among competing feudal lords refereed by an arbitrating *huangdi* to the beginning of an empirewide power struggle based on class interests. Since people were no longer dependent on their feudal lords for achieving the state of nirvana, they no longer felt inseparably bound to their lords in secular life. Gradually, merchants in the service of a particular feudal lord found stronger common interest with other merchants in the service of competing lords than their traditional commitment to clannish feudal loyalty. Before long, the same became true for farmers, scholars, artisans and other tradesmen. And with the tacit encouragement of expanding central power, people began to look to the *huangdi* as a higher authority to champion universal justice and to protect their separate class interests. They also looked to Buddhism to enhance the moral posture of class solidarity against the Confucian demand for absolute hierarchical loyalty toward their local lords. Thus the spread of Buddhism ushered in an age of strong central imperial authority on top of traditional feudalism with local autonomy. Through the spread of Buddhism, an empirewide standard now overshadowed fragmented local autonomy on basic issues of proper human relationship, justice and social order.

Simultaneously, however, Buddhist insistence on a clear separation of ecclesiastical authority from secular control caused constant conflict between the central authority of the dragon throne and independent-minded Buddhist fundamentalists. This conflict was exploited by freewheeling members of *guizu* (the aristocracy) for secular political purposes, particularly those in the south, where greater physical distance from the capital translated into greater local autonomy.

The intellectual role of Buddhist institutions grew increasingly significant and pervasive in Chinese culture. *Sengs* (Buddhist monks) of various sects, in addition to their religious undertakings, took to routinely writing philosophy, conducting schools and keeping libraries. The independence of Buddhist teaching from forbidding Confucian scholasticism was an important factor in Buddhism's popular flowering in China. Buddhist curricula were admittedly overburdened with time-consuming, mind-boggling theological studies, but the discipline acquired from such study methods more than compensated for the heavy investment in time and effort.

Excellence in exegesis requires scholarship, research methodology, creative logic and secular evidential verification, qualities that learned *sengs* cultivated. Buddhist *seng*-scholars soon dominated the fields of mathematics, alchemy, medicine, astronomy and engineering. Buddhist impact on Chinese philosophy was fundamental, introducing new concepts, abstract terms and new words for the description and manipulation of previously unfathomable ideas. Buddhism's influence in Chinese art, architecture and literature was undeniably crucial. Such influence in Tang helped liberate Chinese culture from Confucianism's stultifying repression, particularly on new and creative ideas, much as Western scientific methods would 12 centuries later.

In literature, Buddhist *sutras (fojing),* which were more widely circulated and popularly read than abstruse and elitist Confucian classics, paved the way for other new and lengthy secular literary works, and prepared the reading public for acceptance of mixing prose with verse, for handling of multi-dimensional themes and, ultimately, for the birth of new literary genres such as the novel and drama.

Buddhist understanding of history and of the art of statecraft challenged the staid monopoly of orthodox Confucianism on politics. And Buddhists were increasingly recognized for relative objectivity in their judgment of history and for innovative originality in their approach to secular problems. In both military strategy and political theory, Buddhist intellectual contributions played major roles in a fragmented China's quest for reunification. In return, Buddhism flourished under those rulers, such as those of the Sui Dynasty (581-618), who were wise enough to employ universally potent Buddhist ideas and apply them to political advantage, let alone exploiting ready-made, broad-based support of mushrooming Buddhist communities all over the fragmented political landscape.

The development of China's culture, politics and spirit cannot be fully understood without taking into account the influence of Buddhism since its importation around 2 BC. From the 5th century AD on, Buddhists both contributed to, and in turn were affected by, the historic polarization in China during the era of North-South Dynasties (Nan-Bei Chao 420-589), a period spanning the late phase of Six Dynasties (Liu Chao 220-589) that emerged after the fall of the glorious Han Dynasty (206 BC-AD 220) four centuries previously. Buddhism adapted itself during this period in the south to a society characterized by the independence of a transplanted *guizu* (aristocracy), with large estates of client groups. Its ecclesiastical structure developed into a network of loosely connected, but individually autonomous, monasteries.

It was therefore not surprising that the great southern *seng* (Buddhist monk) Huiyun (334-416) wrote an anti-Confucian essay titled "Treatise on the Exemption of Religious Institutions from Monarchial Authority" *(Shamen bujing Wangzhi Lun)*. Written in 404, the treatise asserted the independence of religion from secular control. It was among the earliest intellectual treatises on the principle of separation of church and state. During the era of North-South Dynasties,

67

traditional central political authority in the north forced Buddhism to seek support from the ruling sovereign, who tended to be the sole source of secular favors.

For example, with transparent motive and shrewd purpose, Seng Fakuo (died 420) of the Bei Wei Dynasty (Northern Wei 386-534), leader of the Buddhist clergy in the north, claimed Emperor Daowu (reigned 386-409) as the living reincarnation of Buddha. Seng Fakuo was bestowed high secular titles during his life, culminating with a hereditary rank of lord. Buddhists of 7th-century China sought favoritism from the secular state at the same time they asserted their independence and separation from traditional imperial institutions by calling for Buddhist exemption from taxation, military service and the long arm of secular law. This inherently contradictory posture still would not have brought the wrath of the dragon throne on Buddhists if they had not been simultaneously engaged in secular factional intrigues and class politics.

Furthermore, growing abuse of religious privileges and laxity in monastic discipline inevitably forced the dragon throne to adopt intrusive measures of control on theology, and secular supervision of ecclesiastic establishments. Also, proliferation of clerical ordination and monasterial founding, much of which was less than legitimate if not outright fraudulent, began to deprive the state of much-needed manpower and tax revenue. The removal from the economy of large tracts of prime land that would be donated outright, or under formulas of deferred giving, or sometimes through fraudulent, tax-evading schemes, caused serious economic imbalance in many areas. The sanctuary provided by Buddhist monasteries to the lawless, to tax evaders and conscript dodgers, as well as to political dissidents, also threatened the totalitarian authority of the dragon throne and security interests of the secular order. The huge expense of Buddhist temple construction, the costly maintenance of an ever-expanding clergy population and its associated lay communities and the drain on the scarce supply of metal caused by the casting of ever larger and larger Buddhist statues and bells interfered with the secular state's own increasingly ambitious plans for domestic capital construction and for arms production needed by foreign conquest.

The growing economic power of Buddhist monasteries, often the main socio-economic institutions in many regions, also had destabilizing political implications. While Buddhism was repeatedly sponsored by secular authorities for political purposes, official anti-Buddhist pogroms, known as *shatai* (ecclesiastical cleansing), systematically recurred throughout the long history of China. This continued up to the Christian-supported 1911 Democratic Revolution that established the Nationalist Republic, not to mention the subsequent Marxist-Leninist People's Republic, particularly during the Cultural Revolution of 1966-76. The distressing phenomenon of *shatai* became even more complex when other issues, such as xenophobia, backlash from social reform, and preventive suppression of political revolts mingled with traditional socio-political pressure for curbing Buddhist expansion into the secular world. State persecution and state sponsorship of religion proved always to be two sides of the same evil coin.

Gunnar Myrdal (1898-1984), Swedish sociologist-economist, in his 1944 definitive study *The American Dilemma,* for which he received the 1974 Nobel Prize for Economics, having declared the "Negro" problem in the United States to be inextricably entwined with the democratic functioning of American society, went on to produce a 1976 study of *Southeast Asia: The Asian Dilemma.* In it he identified Buddhist acceptance of suffering as the prime cause for economic underdevelopment in the region. Myrdal's conclusion would appear valid superficially, given the coincidence of an indisputable existence of conditions of poverty in the region at the time of his study and the pervasive influence of Buddhism in Southeast Asian culture, until the question is asked as to why, whereas Buddhism has dominated Southeast Asia for more than a millennium, pervasive poverty in the region only made its appearance after the arrival of Western imperialism in the 19th century.

Marxists and nationalists, many of both professing no love for Buddhism, suggested that Myrdal had been influenced in his convenient conclusion by his eagerness to deflect responsibility for the sorry state of affairs in the region from the legacy of Western imperialism. As theological apologists tried to rationalize social misery with an accommodating theology to capture the appreciation of the secular polity, Myrdal, social scientist, tried to blame indigenous religion for the sins of secular geopolitics. That which Western scholars identify as the process of modernity appears to have occurred in China's history more than once.

70

Chapter 4 - THE ABDUCTION OF MODERNITY Part 3: Rule of Law vs. Confucianism

The rule of law has been touted frequently by Western scholars as a central aspect of modernity. According to that measure of periodization, since the rule of law was the basis of the first unification of China in the 2nd century BC, modernity occurred 23 centuries ago in China.

Researchers have pointed out that at the end of the 17th century, while the Chinese empire often appeared in English literature as a metaphor for "tyranny", such as in the works of Daniel Defoe, best known for his 1719 novel *Robinson Crusoe,* it was also at times praised for its legal code long established on ideals of order, morality, and good government, such as in the work of Lady Mary Chudleigh, to the more uniform perception of China's legal system at the turn of the century, when George Henry Mason published *The Punishments of*

China (1801). Michel Foucault's analytical approach to history highlights the limitations of European efforts to comprehend China's moral, juridical and legal structures.

The promulgation of a new edition of law, known as the Tang Code of Perpetual Splendor *(Tang Yonghui Lu)*, in the 10th lunar month in the fourth year of the reign of Perpetual Splendor *(Yonghui)* of the Tang Dynasty, in AD 653, was in reality just an update effort, based on the original Tang Code *(Tang Lu)*, which in turn was based on the Sui Code *(Sui Lu)*, which had initially been compiled 73 years earlier by the late founding Civil Emperor *(Wendi)* of the preceding Sui Dynasty and updated ever since by every succeeding sovereign. But the Tang Code of Perpetual Splendor is singled out by history, mostly because of its definitive comprehensiveness.

The original Tang Code was promulgated 29 years earlier, in 624, by the founding High Grand Emperor *(Gaozu)* of the Tang Dynasty. It would become in modern times the earliest fully preserved legal code in the history of Chinese law. It was endowed with a commentary, known as *Tanglu Shuyi*, incorporated in 653, the fourth year of the reign of Perpetual Splendor, as part of the Tang Code of Perpetual Splendor.

The Tang Code was based on the Code of Northern Zhou *(Bei Zhou Lu*, 557-581), promulgated 89 years earlier in 564, which was in turn based on the earlier, less comprehensive and less elaborate Code of Cao Wei *(Cao Wei Lu*, 220-265) and the Code of Western Jin *(Xi Jin Lu*,

265-317) promulgated almost four centuries earlier in 268.

Western perception on the alleged underdevelopment of law in Chinese civilization is based on both factual ignorance and cultural bias. Chinese dismissal of the rule of law is not a rejection of modernity, but a rejection of primitiveness. Confucian attitude places low reliance on law and punishment for maintaining social order. Evidence of this can be found in the Aspiration *(Zhi)* section of the 200-volume *Old Book on Tang (Jiu Tang Shu)*, a magnum opus of Tang historiography. The history classic was compiled under official supervision in 945 during the Late Jin Dynasty *(Hou Jin, 936-946)* of the era of Five Generations *(Wudai, 907-960)*, some three centuries after the actual events. A single chapter on Punishment and Law *(Xingfa)* places last after seven chapters on Rites *(Liyi)*, after which come four chapters on Music *(Yinyue)*, three chapters on Calendar *(Li)*, two on Astronomy and Astrology *(Tianwen)*, one on Physics *(Wuheng)*, four on Geography *(Dili)*, three on Hierarchy of Office *(Zhiguan)*, one on Carriages and Costume *(Yufu)*, two on Sutras and Books *(Jingji)*, two on Commodities *(Chihuo)* and finally comes a single chapter Punishment and Law, in that order.

The Confucian Code of Rites *(Liji)* is expected to be the controlling document on civilized behavior, not law. In the Confucian worldview, rule of law is applied only to those who have fallen beyond the bounds of civilized behavior. Civilized people are expected to observe proper rites. Only social outcasts are expected to have their actions controlled by law. Thus the rule of law is considered a state of barbaric primitiveness, prior to achieving the civilized state of voluntary observation of proper rites. What is legal is not necessarily moral or just.

Under the supervision of Tang Confucian minister Fang Xuanling, 500 sections of ancient laws were compiled into 12 volumes in the Tang Code, titled:

Vol 1: Term and Examples (Mingli)
Vol 2: Security and Forbiddance (Weijin)
Vol 3: Office and Hierarchy (Zhizhi)
Vol 4: Domestic Matters and Marriage (Huhun)
Vol 5: Stables and Storage (Jiuku)
Vol 6: Impeachment and Promotion (Shanxing)
Vol 7: Thievery and Robbery (Zeidao)
Vol 8: Contest and Litigation (Dousong)
Vol 9: Deceit and Falsehood (Zhawei)
Vol 10: Miscellaneous Regulation (Zalu)
Vol 11: Arrest and Escape (Buwang)
Vol 12: Judgment and Imprisonment (Duanyu)

The Tang Code lists five forms of corporal punishment:

1. Flogging *(Chi)*
2. Caning *(Zhang)*
3. Imprisonment *(Tu)*
4. Exile *(Liu)*
5. Death *(Si)*

Leniency is applied to Eight Considerations *(Bayi)*:

1. Blood relation
2. Motive for the crime

3. Virtue of the culprit
4. Ability of the culprit
5. Past merits
6. Nobility status
7. Friendship
8. Diligent character

Criminals above age 90 and those under age seven received only suspended sentences. For others, sentences could be redeemed by cash payments. A death sentence was worth 120 catties of copper coins (1 catty = 1.33 pounds). Officials were entitled to discounts on sentences on private civil offenses: those of Fifth Ranks and above were entitled to a reduction of two years; those of ninth rank and above were entitled to one year; but for public crimes, an additional year was added to the sentence for all officials.

Exempt from leniency are 10 Categories of Wickedness *(Shiwu)*:

1. Conspiratorial sedition *(moufan)*
2. Conspiratorial grand rebellion *(moudani)*
3. Conspiratorial insubordination *(moupan)*
4. Conspiratorial vicious rebelliousness *(moueni)* 5. Immorality *(budao)*
6. Disrespectfulness *(bujing)*
7. Deficiency in filial virtue *(buxiao)*
8. Antisocial behavior *(bulu)*
9. Unrighteousness and disloyalty *(buyi)*
10. Instigation of internal chaos *(neiluan)*

The Chinese term for "law" is *fa-lu.* The word *fa* means "method". The word *lu* means "standard". In other words, law is a methodical standard for behavior in society. A musical instrument with resonant tubes that form the basis of musical scales, the Chinese equivalent of the tuning fork, is also called *lu.* In law, the word *lu* implies a standard scale for measuring social behavior of civilized men.

The first comprehensive code of law in China had been compiled by the Origin Qin Emperor (*Qin Shihuangdi,* reigned 246-210 BC), unifier of China. Known as the Qin Code *(Qin Lu),* it was a political instrument as well as a legal one. It was the legislative manifestation of a Legalist political vision. It aimed at instituting uniform rules for prescribing appropriate social behavior in a newly unified social order. It sought to substitute fragmented traditional local practices, left from the ancient regime of privileged aristocratic lineages. It tried to dismantle Confucian exemptions accorded to special relationships based on social hierarchies and clan connections.

The pervasive growth of new institutions in the unifying Qin Dynasty (221-207 BC) was the result of objective needs of a rising civilization. Among these new institutions was a unified legal system of impartial rewards and punishments according to well-promulgated and clearly defined codes of prescribed behavior. The law was enforced through the practice of *lianzuo* (linked seats), a form of social control by imposing criminal liability on the perpetrator's clan members, associates and friends. Qin culture heralded the later emergence of a professional *shidafu* (literati-bureaucrat) based on meritocracy. It also introduced a uniform system of weights, measures and monetary instruments and it established standard trade practices for the smooth operation of a unified economic system for the whole empire. The effect of Qin Legalist governance on Chinese political culture pushed Chinese civilization a great step forward toward forging an unified nation and culture, but in the process lost much of the richness of its ancient, local traditions and rendered many details of its fragmented past incomprehensible to posterity.

In the first half of the Han Dynasty (206 BC-AD 220), the Han imperial government adopted the Legalist policies of the Qin Dynasty it had replaced. It systemically expanded its power over tribal *guizu* by wholesale adaptation of Legalist political structure from the brief (15 years) but consequential reign of the preceding Qin Dynasty. Gradually, with persistent advice from Confucian ministers, in obsessive quest for dependable political loyalty to the Han dynastic house, Legalist policies of equal justice for all were abandoned in favor of Confucian tendencies of formalized exemptions from law, cemented with special relationships *(guanxi)* based on social positions and kinship. The Tang Code, promulgated in AD 624, institutionalized this Confucian trend by codifying it. It would lay the foundation for a hierarchal social structure that would generate a political culture that would resist the proposition that all men are created equal to mean similarity. In Confucian culture, civilized man is created as closely connected individuals to form building blocks of society. It is the universality of man that celebrates individualism, not the Western notion of alienation as individualism.

Elaborately varied degrees of punishment are accorded by the Tang Code to the same crime committed by persons of different social stations, just as Confucian rites ascribe varying lengths of mourning periods to the survivors of the deceased of various social ranks. According to Confucian logic, if the treatment for death, the most universal of fates, is not socially equal, why should it be for the treatment for crime? William Blake (1757-1827), born 23 centuries after Confucius (551-479 BC), would epitomize the problem of legal fairness in search for true justice, by his famous pronouncement: "One law for the lion and the ox is oppression." Confucians are not against the concept of equal justice for all; they merely have a sophisticated notion of the true meaning of justice.

In Chinese history, the entrenched political feudal order relies on the philosophical concepts of Confucianism *(Ru Jia)*. The rising agricultural capitalistic order draws on the ideology of Legalism *(Fa Jia)*. These two philosophical postures, Confucianism and Legalism, in turn construct alternative and opposing moral contexts, each providing rationalization for the ultimate triumph of its respective sponsoring social order.

The struggle between these two competing social orders has been going on, with alternating periods of triumph for each side, since the Legalist Qin Dynasty first united China in 221 BC, after 26 years of unification war. The effect of this struggle was still visible in the politics of contemporary China, particularly during the Great Proletariat Cultural Revolution of 1966-78, when the Gang of Four promoted Legalist concepts to attack the existing order, accusing it of being Confucian in philosophy and counterrevolutionary in ideology. To the extent that "left" and "right" convey meaningful images in modern political nomenclature, Taoism *(Dao Jia)* would be to the left of Confucianism as Legalism would be to the right.

Modern Legalists in China, such as the so-called Gang of Four, were the New Left, whose totalitarian zeal to promote social justice converged, in style if not in essence, with the New Right, or neo-conservatives of the West, in its reliance on authoritarian zeal to defend individualism. Thus the notion that modernity is a Western phenomenon is highly problematic. **Ah, Liu**

79

finally admits that individualism is not only the product of the West!

The flowering of Chinese philosophy in the 5th century BC was not accidental. By that time, after the political disintegration of the ancient Xi Zhou Dynasty (Western Zhou, 1027-771 BC), Chinese society was at a crossroads in its historical development. Thus an eager market emerged for various rival philosophical underpinnings to rationalize a wide range of different, competing social systems. The likes of Confucius were crisscrossing the fragmented political landscape of petty independent kingdoms, seeking fame and fortune by hawking their moral precepts and political programs to ambitious and opportunistic   monarchs.

Traditionally, members of the Chinese *guizu* (the aristocracy) were descendants of hero warriors who provided meritorious service to the founder of a dynasty. Relatives of *huangdi* (the emperor), provided they remained in political good graces, also became aristocrats by birthright, although technically they were members of *huangzu* (the imperial clan). The emperor lived in constant fear of this *guizu* class, more than he feared the peasants, for *guizu* members had the means and political ambition for successful coups. Peasant uprisings in Chinese history have been rare, only seven uprisings in 4,000 years of recorded history up to the modern time. Moreover, these uprisings have tended to aim at local abuse of power rather than at central authority. Aristocratic coups, on the other hand, have been countless and frequent.

In four millennia, Chinese history recorded 559 emperors. Approximately one-third of them suffered violent deaths from aristocratic plots, while none had been executed by rebelling peasants.

The political function of the emperor was to keep peace and order among contentious nobles and to protect peasants from aristocratic abuse. This was the basic rationale of government as sovereign. A sovereign, whether an emperor or a president, without the loyal support of peasants, euphemistically referred to as the Mandate of Heaven *(Tianming)*, would soon find himself victim of a palace coup or aristocratic revolt. This is the socialist root of all governments. The neo-liberal claim of the proper role of government as ensuring a free market is a capitalist cooptation of government.

The Code of Rites *(Liji)*, the ritual compendium as defined by Confucius, circumscribed acceptable personal behavior for all in a hierarchical society. It established rules of appropriate socio-political conduct required in a feudal civilization. Unfortunately, ingrained conditioning by conservative Confucian teaching inevitably caused members of the aristocratic class to degenerate in time from truly superior stock into mediocre and decadent seekers of unearned privileges. Such degeneration was brought about by the nature of their privileged life and the false security derived from a Confucian superiority complex. Although the process might sometimes take centuries to take shape, some dynasties would crumble within decades through the unchecked excesses of their ruling classes.

Confucianism, by promoting unquestioning loyalty toward authority, encouraged the powerful to abuse their power, despite Confucianism's reliance on ritual morality as a mandate for power. Confucianism is therefore inescapably the victim of its own success, as Taoists are fond of pointing out.

Generally, those who feel they can achieve their political objectives without violence would support the Code of Rites. While those whose political objectives are beyond the reach of non-violent, moral persuasion would dismiss it as a tool of oppression. Often, those who attacked the Code of Rites during their rise to power would find it expedient to promote, after achieving power, the very code they belittled before, since they soon realized that the Code of Rites was the most effective governing tool for a sitting ruler.

To counter hostile tendencies toward feudal values and to ensure allegiance to the feudal system, *keju* (civil examinations), while providing equal opportunity to all talented, were designed to test candidates on their knowledge of a syllabus of Confucian doctrines contained in the Five Classics *(Wujing)*. Confucian ethics were designed to buttress the terms of traditional social contract. They aimed to reduce potential for violent conflict between the arrived and the arriving. They aimed to channel the powerful energy of the arriving into a constructive force for social renewal. Confucian ethics aimed to forge in perpetuity a continuing non-violent dialectic eclecticism, to borrow a Hegelian term for the benefit of Western comprehension.

The violent overthrow of the government, a criminal offense in the United States, is a moral sin in Confucian ethics. It is therefore natural that budding revolutionaries should attack Confucian ethics as reactionary, and that those already in power should tirelessly promote Confucian ethics as the only proper code of behavior for a self-renewing, civilized socio-political order. In Chinese politics, Confucianism is based on a theory of rule by self-restraint. It advocates the sacredness of hierarchy and the virtue of loyalty. It is opposed by Legalism, which subscribes to a theory of rule by universal law and impartial enforcement. Again, the Western claim that the rule of law is a unique foundation of modernity peculiar to the West is historically unsubstantiated.

Although Buddhists have their own disagreements with Legalist concepts, particularly on the issue of mercy, which they value as a virtue while Legalists detest it as the root of corruption, such disagreements are muted by Buddhist appreciation of Legalist opposition to both Confucianism and Taoism, ideological nemeses of Buddhism *(Fo Jiao)*. Above all, Buddhists need for their own protection Legalism's opposition to selective religious persecution. Legalism, enemy of Buddhism's enemies, is selected by Buddhists as a convenient ally.

Legalism places importance on three aspects. The first is *shi* (authority), which is based on the legitimacy of the ruler and the doctrinal orthodoxy of his policies. The second is *shu* (skill) in manipulative exercise of power, and the third is *fa* (law), which, once publicly proclaimed, should govern universally without exceptions. These three aspects Legalists consider as three pillars of a well-governed society. If the rule of law is a characteristic of modernity, then modernity arrived in China in 3rd century BC.

According to Confucian political theory, the essential political function of all subjects is to serve the emperor, not personally, but as sovereign, who is the sole legitimate personification of the political order and sovereign of the political realm. Legalists argue that while all powers emanate by right from the Son of Heaven, the proper execution of these powers can take place only within an impartial system of law. While people should be taught their ritual responsibilities, they should at the same time be held responsible by law not only for each person's individual acts but also for one another's conducts, as an extensive form of social control within a good community. Therefore, punishment should be meted out to not only the culprit, but also to his relatives, friends, associates and neighbors, for negligence of their ritual duties in constraining the culprit. This is natural for a society in which the individual is inseparable from community.

Efficiency of government and equal justice for all are cardinal rules of good politics. Legalists believe that administration of the state should be entrusted to officials appointed according to merit, rather than to hereditary nobles or literati with irrelevant scholarship. Even granting validity to the extravagant Taoist claim that ideas, however radical, are inherently civilized and noble, Legalists insist that when ideas are transformed into unbridled action, terror, evil, vulgarity and destruction emerge. Freedom of thought must be balanced by rule of law to restrain the corruption of ideas by action.

Whereas being well versed in Confucianism bound the *shidafu* class culturally as faithful captives to the imperial system, such rigid mentality ironically also rendered its subscribers indifferent to objective problem-solving. Thus Confucianism, by its very nature, would ensure eventual breakdown of the established order, at which point Legalism would gain ascendancy for a period, to put in place new policies and laws that would be more responsive to objective conditions. But Confucians took comfort in the fact that, in time, the new establishment that Legalists put in charge would discover the utilitarian advantage of Confucianism to the ruling elite. And the cycle of conservative consolidation would start once again. Generally, periods of stability and steady decay would last longer than intervals of violent renewal through Legalist reform, so that Confucianism would become more ingrained after each cycle. Western capitalism is in essence a feudal system, supported by a legal system that legitimizes property rights and class distinction based on private capital ownership. In contemporary Chinese political nomenclature, the proletariat is defined not merely as workers, but the property-less class.

This perpetual, cyclical development proves to the Taoist mind that indeed "life goes in circles". It is an astute observation made by the ancient sage Laozi, father of Taoism, who lived during the 6th century BC and who was the alleged ancestor of the Tang imperial clan of 7th century AD.

The so-called Gang of Four promoted Legalist politics in China in the 1970s. They used Marxist orthodox doctrine, reinforced by the Maoist personality cult, as *shi* (influence), Communist party discipline as *shu* (skill) for exercising power, and dictatorial rule as *fa* (laws) to be obeyed with no exceptions allowed for tradition, ancient customs or special relationships and with little regard for human conditions. Legalists yearn for a perfectly administered state, even if the price is the unhappiness of its citizens. They seek an inviolable system of impartial justice, without extenuating allowances, even at the expense of the innocent. When *a priori* truth appears threatened by fidelity in logic, Confucians predictably always rely on faithful loyalty to tradition as a final argument.

Confucius, the quintessential conservative, the most influential philosopher in Chinese culture, admired the idealized society of the ancient Xi Zhou Dynasty, when men purportedly lived in harmony under sage rulers.

The fact that the Zhou Dynasty had been a feudal society based on slavery did not concern Confucius. To the idealist Confucius, hierarchical stations in human society were natural and symbiotic. If everyone would contentedly do his duty according to his particular station in society, and with an accepting state of mind known as *anfen,* then all men would benefit as social life meliorates toward an ideal state of high civilization.

To Confucius, the lot of a slave in a good society was preferable to that of a lord in a society marked by chaos and uncivilized immorality. Violent social changes would only create chaos, which would bring decay and destruction to all, lords and slaves alike. Such violent changes would kill the patient in the process of fighting the disease. Confucius apparently never sought the opinion of any slave on this matter.

Like Plato, Confucius conceived a world in which the timeless ideal of morality constitutes the perfect reality, of which the material world is but a flawed reflection.

The Zhou people, according to Confucius - in stark contrast to historical fact - aspired to be truthful, wise, good and righteous. They allegedly observed meticulously their social ritual obligation *(li)* and with clear understanding of the moral content of such rites. Confucius never explained why the Zhou people failed so miserably in their noble aspirations, or the cause of their eventual fall from civilized grace.

In the Confucian world view, men have degenerated since the fall of the Zhou Dynasty. As a result of barbarian invasions of Chinese society and of natural atrophy, social order has broken down. But, being fundamentally good, men can be salvaged through education, the key to which is moral examples, emanating from the top, because the wisest in an ideal society would naturally rise to the top. And they have a responsibility to teach the rest of society by the examples of their moral behavior.

Chinese audiences always enjoy hearing that greatness in Chinese culture is indigenous while decadence is solely the influence of foreign barbarians. Collective self-criticism, unlike xenophobia, has never been a favorite Chinese preoccupation. Chinese narcissism differs from Western narcissism in that superiority is based not on physical power but on social benevolence. From the Chinese historical perspective, the defeat of civilized Athens at the hand of militant Sparta set the entire Western civilization on the wrong footing. It represented the triumph of barbarism from which the West has never recovered.

The Zhou people that Confucius idolized traced their ancestry to the mythical deity Houji, god of agriculture. This genealogical claim had no factual basis in history. Rather, it had been invented by the Zhou people to mask their barbaric origin as compared with the superior culture of the preceding Shang Dynasty (1600-1028 BC), which they had conquered and whose culture they had appropriated, just as the Romans invented Aeneas, mythical Trojan hero, son of Anchises and Venus, as father of their lineage to give themselves an ancestor as cultured and ancient as those of the more sophisticated Greeks. The Tang imperial house was at least humble enough to coopt only Laozi, a real historical figure rather than a god.

The historic figure responsible for the flowering of Zhou culture was Ji Dan, Duke of Zhou, known reverently as Zhougong in Chinese. Zhougong was the third-ranking brother of the founding Martial King (Wuwang, 1027-1025 BC) of the Zhou Dynasty. The Martial King claimed to be a 17th-generation descendant of the god Houji, who allegedly gave the Chinese people the gift of agriculture. In Chinese politics, appropriation of mythical celebrities as direct ancestors of political rulers started long before the claim by the Tang imperial house on Laozi, founder of Taoism.

Zhougong introduced to Chinese politics the practice of hereditary monarchy based on the principle of primogeniture. He put an end to the ancient tribal custom of the Shang Dynasty of crowning the next younger brother of a deceased king.

In defiance of established tradition, after the death of the Martial King (Wuwang) of the Zhou Dynasty in 1025 BC, Zhougong, third-ranking brother, arranged to usurp the dragon throne for his nephew, Cheng Wang, 12-year-old son of the deceased Martial King. The move bypassed Zhougong's older, second-ranking brother, Ji Guanxu, the legitimate traditional heir according to ancient tribal custom. Ji Guanxu rebelled in protest to defend his legitimate right to succeed his deceased older brother. But he was defeated and killed in battle by Zhougong.

Hereditary monarchy based on the principle of primogeniture as established by Zhougong has since been viewed by historians as the institution that launched modern political statehood out of primitive tribal nationhood. It has been credited with having fundamentally advanced Chinese civilization. Modernity began with the nation-state, and in China that transition occurred more than a millennium before the birth of Christ.

Having acted as regent for seven years on behalf of Cheng Wang (1024-1005 BC), his under-aged nephew king, the fratricidal Zhougong returned political power, some would say involuntarily, to the fully grown Cheng Wang. The descendants of Cheng Wang upheld hereditary monarchy in the Zhou Dynasty for three more centuries and firmly established primogeniture as an unquestioned tradition in Chinese political culture.

Zhougong gave Chinese civilization the Five Rites and the Six Categories of Music, which form the basis of civilization. Confucian idealism manifests human destiny in a civilization rooted in morality as defined by the Code of Rites, without which man would revert back to the state of wild beasts. Zhougong was credited with having established feudalism as a socio-political order during his short regency of only seven years. He institutionalized it with an elaborate system of Five Rites *(Wuli)* that has survived the passage of time.

The Five Rites are:

1. Rites governing social relationships
2. Rites governing behavioral codes
3. Rites governing codes of dress
4. Rites governing marriage
5. Rites governing burial practices

He also established Six Categories of Music *(Liuluo)* for all ritual occasions, giving formal ceremonial expression to social hierarchy. Confucius revered Zhougong as the father of formal Chinese feudal culture. The son of Zhougong, by the name of Ji Baqin, had been bestowed the First Lord of the State of Lu by Cheng Wang (1024-1005 BC), second-generation ruler of the Zhou dynasty who owed his dragon throne to Zhougong, his third-ranking uncle. Five centuries later, the State of Lu became the adopted home of Confucius, who had been born in the State of Song.

However, the pragmatic descendants of Zhougong in the State of Lu did not find appealing the revivalist advice of Confucius, even when such advice had been derived from the purported wisdom of Zhougong, their illustrious ancestor. Confucius, as an old sage, had to peddle his moralist ideas in other neighboring states for a meager living. In despair, Confucius, the frustrated rambling philosopher, was recorded to have lamented in resignation: "It has been too long since I last visited Zhougong in my dreams."

The essential idea underlying the political thinking in Confucian philosophy is that fallen men require the control of repressive institutions to restore their innate potential for goodness. According to Confucius, civilization is the inherent purpose of human life, not conquest. To advance civilization is the responsibility of the wise and the cultured, both individually and collectively. Enlightened individuals should teach ignorant individuals. Cultured nations should bring civilization to savage tribes.

A superior ruler should cultivate qualities of a virtuous man. His virtue would then influence his ministers around him. They in turn would be examples to others of lower ranks, until all men in the realm are permeated with noble, moral aptitude. The same principle of trickle-down morality would apply to relations between strong and weak nations and between advanced and developing cultures and economies.

THE WHITE MAN'S BURDEN

Rudyard Kipling's notion of "the white man's burden" would be Confucian in principle, provided that one agrees with his interpretation of the "superiority" of the white man's culture. Modern Confucians would consider Kipling (1865-1936) as having confused Western material progress with moral superiority, as measured by a standard based on virtue.

Confucius would have thoroughly approved of the ideas put forth by Plato (427-347 BC) in the *Republic,* in which a philosopher king rules an ideal kingdom where all classes happily go about performing their prescribed separate socio-economic functions.

Taoists would comment that if only life were so neat and simple, there would be no need for philosophy.

Confucian ideas have aspects that are similar to Christian beliefs, only down side up. Christ taught the pleasure-seeking and power-craving Greco-Roman world to love the weak and imitate the poor, whose souls were proclaimed as pure. Confucius taught the materialistic

Chinese to admire the virtuous and respect the highly placed, whose characters were presumed to be moral.

The word *ren,* a Chinese term for human virtue, means "proper human relationship". Without exact equivalent in English, the word *ren* is composed by combining the ideogram "man" with the numeral 2, a concept necessitated by the plurality of mankind and the quest for proper interpersonal relationship. It is comparable to the Greek concept of humanity and the Christian notion of divine love, the very foundation of Christianity.

Confucius' well-known admonition, "Do not unto others that which you not wish to have done to yourself," has been frequently compared with Christ's teaching, "Love thy neighbor as thyself."

Both lead to the same end, but from opposite directions. Confucius was less intrusively interfering but, of course, unlike Christ, he had the benefit of having met Laozi, founder of Taoism and consummate proponent of benign non-interference. A close parallel was proclaimed by Hillel (30 BC-AD 10), celebrated Jewish scholar and president of the Sanhedrin, in his famous maxim: "Do not unto others that which is hateful unto thee."

By observing rites of Five Relationships, each individual would clearly understand his social role, and each would voluntarily behave according to proper observance of rites that meticulously define such relationships.

No reasonable man would challenge the propriety of the Five Relationships *(Wulun)*. It is the most immutable fixation of cultural correctness in Chinese consciousness.

The Five Relationships *(Wulun)* governed by Confucian rites are those of:

1. Sovereign to subject
2. Parent to child
3. Elder to younger brother
4. Husband to wife
5. Friend to friend

These relationships form the basic social structure of Chinese society. Each component in the relationships assumes ritual obligations and responsibility to the others at the same time he or she enjoys privileges and due consideration accorded by the other components.

Confucius would consider heretical the ideas of Jean Jacques Rousseau (1721-28), who would assert two millennia after Confucius that man is good by nature but is corrupted by civilization.

Confucius would argue that without a Code of Rites *(Liji)* for governing human behavior, as embedded in the ritual compendium defined by him based on the ideas of Zhougong, human beings would be no better than animals, which Confucius regarded with contempt. Love of animals, a Buddhist notion, is an alien concept to Confucians, who proudly display their species prejudice.

Confucius acknowledged man to be benign by nature but, in opposition to Rousseau, he saw man's goodness only as an innate potential and not as an inevitable characteristic. To Confucius, man's destiny lies in his effort to elevate himself from savagery toward civilization in order to fulfill his potential for good.

The ideal state rests on a stable society over which a virtuous and benevolent sovereign/emperor rules by moral persuasion based on a Code of Rites rather than by law. Justice would emerge from a timeless morality that governs social behavior. Man would be orderly out of self-respect for his own moral character rather than from fear of punishment prescribed by law. A competent and loyal literati-bureaucracy *(shidafu)* faithful to a just political order would run the government according to moral principles rather than following rigid legalistic rules devoid of moral content. The behavior of the sovereign is proscribed by the Code of Rites. Nostalgic of the idealized feudal system that purportedly had existed before the Spring and Autumn Period (*Chunqiu,* 770-481 BC) in which he lived, Confucius yearned for the restoration of the ancient Zhou socio-political culture that existed two-and-a-half centuries before his time. He dismissed the objectively different contemporary social realities of his own time as merely symptoms of chaotic degeneration. Confucius abhorred social atrophy and political anarchy. He strove incessantly to fit the real and imperfect world into the straitjacket of his idealized moral image. Confucianism, by placing blind faith on a causal connection between virtue and power, would remain the main cultural obstacle to China's periodic attempts to evolve from a society governed by men into a society governed by law. The danger of Confucianism lies not in its aim to endow the virtuous with power, but in its tendency to label the powerful as virtuous. This is a problem that cannot be solved by the rule of law, since law is generally used by the powerful to control the weak.

Mencius claimed that the Mandate of Heaven was conditioned on virtuous rule. Mencius (Meng-tzu, 371-288 BC), prolific apologist for Confucius, the equivalent embodiment of St Paul and Thomas Aquinas in Confucianism, though not venerated until the 11th century AD during the Song Dynasty (960-1279), greatly contributed to the survival and acceptance of the ideas of Confucius. But Mencius went further. He argued that a ruler's authority is derived from the Mandate of Heaven (Tianming), that such mandate is not perpetual or automatic and that it depends on good governance worthy of a virtuous sovereign.

The concept of a Mandate of Heaven as proposed by Mencius is in fact a challenge to the concept of the divine right of absolute monarchs. The Mandate of Heaven can be lost through the immoral behavior of the ruler, or failings in his responsibility for the welfare of the people, in which case Heaven will grant another, more moral individual a new mandate to found a new dynasty. Loyalty will inspire loyalty. Betrayal will beget betrayal. A sovereign unworthy of his subjects will be rejected by them. Such is the will of Heaven *(Tian)*.

Arthurian legend in medieval lore derived from Celtic myths a Western version of the Chinese Mandate of Heaven. Arthur, illegitimate son of Uther Pendragon, king of Britain, having been raised incognito, was proclaimed king after successfully withdrawing Excalibur, a magic sword embedded in stone allegedly removable only by a true king. Arthur ruled a happy kingdom as a noble king and fair warrior by reigning over a round table of knights in his court at Camelot. But his kingdom lapsed into famine and calamity when he became morally wounded by his abuse of kingly powers. To cure Arthur's festering moral wound, his knights embarked on a quest for the Holy Grail, identified by Christians as the chalice of the Last Supper brought to England by St Joseph of Arimathea.

Mencius' political outlook of imperative heavenly mandate profoundly influences Chinese historiography, the art of official historical recording. It tends to equate ephemeral reigns with immorality. And it associates protracted reigns with good government. It is a hypothesis that, in reality, is neither true nor inevitable.

It is necessary to point out that Mencius did not condone revolutions, however justified by immorality of the ruling political authority or injustice in the contemporary social system. He merely used threat of replacement of one ruler with another more enlightened to curb behavioral excesses of despotism. To Mencius, political immorality was always incidental but never structural. As such, he was a reformist rather than a revolutionary.

Nicolo Machiavelli, in 1512, 18 centuries after Mencius, wrote *The Prince,* which pioneered modern Western political thought by making medieval disputes of legitimacy irrelevant. He detached politics from all pretensions of theology and morality, firmly establishing it as a purely secular activity and opening the door for modern Western political science. Religious thinkers and moral philosophers would charge that Macchiavelli glorified evil and legitimized despotism. Legalists of the Qin Dynasty (221-207 BC), who preceded publication of *The Prince* by 17 centuries, would have celebrated Machiavelli as a champion of truth.

Mencius, an apologist for Confucian ethics, was Machiavellian in his political strategy in that he deduced a virtuous reign as the most effective form of power politics. He advocated a utilitarian theory of morality in politics. A similar view to that of Mencius was advocated by Thomas Hobbes almost two millennia later. Hobbes set down the logic of modern absolutism in his book *Leviathan* (1651). It was published two years after the execution of Charles I, who had been found royally guilty of the high crime of treason by Oliver Cromwell's regicidal Rump Parliament in commonwealth England. Hobbes, while denying all subjects any moral right to resist the sovereign, subscribed to the fall of a sovereign as the utilitarian result of the sovereign's own failure in his prescribed royal obligations.

Revolts are immoral and illegal, unless they are successful revolutions, in which case the legitimacy of the new regime becomes unquestionable. In application to theology, God is the successful devil; or conversely the devil is a fallen god. It is pure Confucian-Mencian logic. As Taoists have pointed out, there are many Confucians who evade the debate on the existence of God, but it is hard to find one who does not find the devil everywhere, particularly in politics.

Confucius, during his lifetime, was ambivalent about the religious needs of the populace. "Respect the spirits and gods to keep them distant," he advised. He also declined a request to elucidate on the supernatural after-life by saying: "Not even knowing yet all there is to know about life, how can one have any knowledge of death?" It was classic evasion.

Confucianism is in fact a secular, anti-religious force, at least in its philosophical constitution. It downgrades other-worldly metaphysics while it cherishes secular

101

utility. It equates holiness with human virtue rather than with godly divinity. According to Confucius, man's salvation lies in his morality rather than his piety. Confucian precepts assert that man's incentive for moral behavior is rooted in his quest for respect from his peers rather than for love from God. This morality abstraction finds its behavioral manifestation through a Code of Rites that defines proper roles and obligations of each individual within a rigidly hierarchical social structure. Confucians are guided by a spiritual satisfaction derived from winning immortal respect from posterity rather than by the promise of everlasting paradise after God's judgment. They put their faith in meticulous observance of secular rites, as opposed to Buddhists, who worship through divine rituals of faith. Confucians tolerate God only if belief in his existence would strengthen man's morality.

Without denying the existence of the supernatural, Confucians assert its irrelevance in this secular world. Since existence of God is predicated on its belief by man, Confucianism, in advocating man's reliance of his own morality, indirectly denies the existence of God by denying its necessity. To preserve social order, Confucianism instead places emphasis on prescribed human behavior within the context of rigid social relationships through the observance of rituals.

As righteousness precludes tolerance and morality permits no mercy, therein lie the oppressive roots of Confucianism. Most religions instill in their adherents fear of a God who is nevertheless forgiving. Confucianism, more a socio-political philosophy than a religion, distinguishes itself by preaching required observation of an inviolable Code of Rites, the secular ritual compendium as defined by Confucius, in which tolerance is considered as decadence and mercy as weakness. Whereas Legalism advocates equality under the law without mercy, Confucianism, though equally merciless, allows varying standards of social behavior in accordance with varying ritual stations. However, such ritual allowances are not to be construed as tolerance for human frailty, for which Confucianism has little use.

St Augustine (354-430) who was born 905 years after Confucius, in systematizing Christian thought defended the doctrines of original sin and the fall of man. He thus reaffirmed the necessity of God's grace for man's salvation, and further formulated the Church's authority as the sole guarantor of Christian faith. The importance of Augustine's contribution to cognition by Europeans of their need for Christianity and to their acceptance of the orthodoxy of the Catholic Church can be appreciated by contrasting his affirmative theological ideas to the anti-religious precepts of Confucius.

Immanuel Kant (1724-1804), who was born 2,275 years after Confucius, developed the theme of "Transcendental Dialectic" in his *Critic of Pure Reason* (1781). Kant asserted that all theoretical attempts to know things inherently, which he called "nounena", beyond observable "phenomena", are bound to fail. Kant showed that the three great problems of metaphysics - God, free will and immortality - are insoluble by speculative thought, and their existence can neither be confirmed nor denied on theoretical grounds, nor can it be rationally demonstrated.

In this respect, Kantian rationalism lies parallel to Confucian spiritual utilitarianism, though each proceeds from opposite premises. Confucius allowed belief in God only as a morality tool. Rationally, Kant declared that the limits of reason only render proof elusive; they do not necessarily negate belief in the existence of God.

Kant went on to claim in his moral philosophy of categorical imperative that existence of morality requires belief in existence of God, free will and immortality, in contrast to the agnostic claims of Confucius.

Buddhism, in its emphasis on a next life through rebirth after God's judgment, resurrected the necessity of God to the Chinese people. Mercy is all in Buddhist doctrine. Buddhist influence put a human face on an otherwise austere Confucian culture. At the same time, Buddhist mercy tended to invite lawlessness in secular society, while Buddhist insistence on God's judgment on a person's secular behavior encroached on the sovereign/emperor's claim of totalitarian authority.

Similar to Confucian-Mencian logic that revolts are immoral and illegal, unless they are successful revolutions in which case the legitimacy of the new regime becomes unquestionable, John Locke in 1680 wrote *Two Treaties of Government,* which was not published until 10 years later, after the Glorious Revolution of 1688, as a justification of a triumphant revolution. According to Locke, men contract to form political regimes to better protect individual rights of life, liberty and estate. Civil power to make laws and police power to execute such laws adequately are granted to government by the governed for the public good. Only when government betrays society's trust may the governed legitimately refuse obedience to government, namely when government invades the inviolable rights of individuals and their civil institutions and degenerates from a government of law to despotism. An unjust king provides the justification for his own overthrow.

Locke, like Mencius two millennia before him, identified passive consent of the governed as a prerequisite of legitimacy for the sovereign. Confucius would insist that consent of the governed is inherent in the Mandate of Heaven for a virtuous sovereign, a divine right conditioned by virtue. In that respect, it differs from unconditional divine right claimed by Louis XIV of France. However, the concept of a Mandate of Heaven has one similarity with the concept of divine right. According to Confucius, just rule is required as a ritual requisite for a moral ruler, rather than a calculated requirement for political survival. Similarly, the Sun King would view good kingship as a character of greatness rather than as a compromise for winning popular support.

Both Hobbes and Locke based their empiricist notions of political legitimacy not on theological or historical arguments, but on inductive theories of human nature and rational rules of social contract. Confucius based his moralist notion of political legitimacy on historical idealism derived from an idealized view of a perfect, hierarchical human society governed by rites.

For Taoists, followers of Laozi, man-made order is arbitrary by definition, and therefore it is always oppressive. Self-governing anarchy would be the preferred ideal society. The only effective way to fight the inevitably oppressive establishment would be to refuse to participate on its terms, thus depriving the establishment of its strategic advantage.

Mao Zedong (1893-1976), towering giant in modern Chinese history, with apt insights on Taoist doctrines, advocated a strategy for defeating a corrupt enemy of superior military strength through guerrilla warfare. The strategy is summed up by the following pronouncement: "You fight yours [*ni-da ni-de*]; I fight mine [*wo-da wo-de*]."

The strategy ordains that, to be effective, guerrilla forces should avoid frontal engagement with stronger and better equipped government regular army. Instead, they should employ unconventional strategies that would exploit advantages inherent in smaller, weaker irregular guerrilla forces, such as ease of movement, invisibility and flexible logistics. Such strategies would include ambushes and harassment raids that would challenge the prestige and undermine the morale of regular forces of the corrupt government. Such actions would expose to popular perception the helplessness of the immoral establishment, despite its superficial massive power, the paper tiger, as Mao would call it. Thus such strategies would weaken the materially-stronger but morally weaker enemy for an eventual *coup de grace* by popular forces of good.

Depriving an immoral enemy's regular army of offensive targets is the first step in a strategy of wearing down a corrupt enemy of superior force. It is classic Taoist *roushu* (flexible methods). Informed of conceptual differences of key schools of Chinese philosophy, one can understand why historiographers in China have always been Confucian. Despite repeat, periodic draconian measures undertaken by Legalist reformers, ranging from the unifying Qin Dynasty (221-207 BC), during whose reign Confucian scholars were persecuted by being buried alive and their books burned publicly, and up to the Legalist period of the so-called Gang of Four in modern times, when Confucian ideas were vilified and suppressed, Confucianism survives and flourishes, often resurrected by its former attackers from both the left and the right, for the victor's own purposes, once power has been secured.

Feudalism in China takes the form of a centralized federalism of autonomous local lords in which the authority of the sovereign is symbiotically bound to, but clearly separated from, the authority of the local lords. Unless the local lords abuse their local authority, the emperor's authority over them, while all-inclusive in theory, would not extend beyond federal matters in practice, particularly if the emperor's rule is to remain moral within its ritual bounds. In that sense, the Chinese empire was fundamentally different than the predatory empires of Western imperialism.

Confucianism, through the Code of Rites, seeks to govern the behavior and obligation of each person, each social class and each socio-political unit in society. Its purpose is to facilitate the smooth functioning and the perpetuation of the feudal system. Therefore, the power of the sovereign/emperor, though politically absolute, is not free from the constraints of behavior deemed proper by Confucian values for a moral sovereign, just as the authority of the local lords is similarly constrained. Issues of constitutionality in the US political milieu become issues of proper rites and befitting morality in Chinese dynastic or even contemporary politics.

Confucian values, because they have been designed to preserve the existing feudal system, unavoidably would run into conflict with contemporary ideas reflective of new emerging social conditions. It is in the context of its inherent hostility toward progress and its penchant for obsolete nostalgia that Confucian values, rather than feudalism itself, become culturally oppressive and socially damaging. When Chinese revolutionaries throughout history, and particularly in the late 18th and early 19th century, would rebel against the cultural oppression of reactionary Confucianism, they would simplistically and conveniently link it synonymously with political feudalism. These revolutionaries would succeed in dismantling the formal governmental structure of political feudalism because it is the more visible target.

109

Their success is due also to the terminal decadence of the decrepit governmental machinery of dying dynasties, such as the ruling house of the three-century-old, dying Qing Dynasty (1583-1911). Unfortunately, these triumphant revolutionaries in politics remained largely ineffective in remolding Confucian dominance in feudal culture, even among the progressive intelligentsia.

Almost a century after the fall of the feudal Qing Dynasty house in 1911, after countless movements of reform and revolution, ranging from Western moderate democratic liberalism to extremist Bolshevik radicalism, China would have yet to find an workable alternative to the feudal political culture that would be intrinsically sympathetic to its social traditions. Chinese revolutions, including the modern revolution that began in 1911, through its various metamorphoses over the span of almost four millennia, in overthrowing successive political regimes of transplanted feudalism, repeatedly killed successive infected patients in the form of virulent governments. But they failed repeatedly to sterilize the infectious virus of Confucianism in its feudal political culture.

The modern destruction of political feudalism produces administrative chaos and social instability in China until the founding of the People's Republic in 1949. But Confucianism still appeared alive and well as cultural feudalism, even under Communist rule. It continued to instill its victims with an instinctive hostility toward new ideas, especially if they were of foreign origin. Confucianism adhered to an ideological rigidity that amounted to blindness to objective problem-solving.

110

Almost a century of recurring cycles of modernization movements, either Nationalist or Marxist, did not manage even a slight dent in the all-controlling precepts of Confucianism in the Chinese mind. Worse, these movements often mistook Westernization as modernization, moving toward militant barbarism as the new civilization.

In fact, in 1928, when the Chinese Communist Party attempted to introduce a soviet system of government by elected councils in areas of northern China under its control, many of the peasants earnestly thought a new "Soviet" dynasty was being founded by a new emperor by the name of So Viet.

During the Great Proletariat Cultural Revolution of 1966, the debate between Confucianism and Legalism was resurrected as allegorical dialogue for contemporary political struggle. At the dawn of the 21st century, Confucianism remained alive and well under both governments on Chinese soil on both sides of the Taiwan Strait, regardless of political ideology. Modern China was still a society in search of an emperor figure and a country governed by feudal relationships, but devoid of a compatible political vehicle that could turn these tenacious, traditional social instincts toward constructive purposes, instead of allowing them to manifest themselves as practices of corruption. The Western notion of rule of law has little to contribute to that search.

General Douglas MacArthur presented post-World War II Japan, which has been seminally influenced by Chinese culture for 14 centuries, with the greatest gift a victor in war has ever presented the vanquished: the retention of its secularized emperor, despite the Japanese emperor's less-than-benign role in planning the war and in condoning war crimes. Thus MacArthur, in preserving a traditional cultural milieu in which democratic political processes could be adopted without the danger of a socio-cultural vacuum, laid the socio-political foundation for Japan as a postwar economic power. There is logic in observing that the aggressive expansion of Japan would not have occurred had the Meiji Restoration not adopted Western modernization as a path to power. It was Japan's aping of British imperialism that launched it toward its militarism that led to its role in World War II. Of the three great revolutions in modern history - the French, the Chinese and the Russian - each overthrew feudal monarchial systems to introduce idealized Western democratic alternatives that would have difficulty holding the country together without periods of terror. The French and Russian Revolutions both made the fundamental and tragic error of revolutionary regicide and suffered decades of social and political dislocation as a result, with little if any socio-political benefit in return. In France, it would not even prevent eventual restoration imposed externally by foreign victors. The Chinese revolution in 1911 was not plagued by regicide, but it prematurely dismantled political feudalism before it had a chance to develop a workable alternative, plunging the country into decades of warlord rule.

Worse still, it left largely undisturbed a Confucian culture while it demolished its political vehicle. The result was that eight decades after the fall the last dynastic house, the culture-bound nation would still be groping for an appropriate and workable political system, regardless of ideology. Mao Zedong understood this problem and tried to combat it by launching the Great Proletariat Cultural Revolution in 1966. But even after a decade of enormous social upheaval, tragic personal sufferings, fundamental economic dislocation and unparalleled diplomatic isolation, the Cultural Revolution would achieve little except serious damage to the nation's physical and socio-economic infrastructure, to the prestige of the Chinese Communist Party, not to mention the loss of popular support, and total bankruptcy of revolutionary zeal among even loyal party cadres.

It would be unrealistic to expect the revival of imperial monarchy in modern China. Once a political institution is overthrown, all the king's men cannot put it together again. Yet the modern political system in China, despite its revolutionary clothing and radical rhetoric, is still fundamentally feudal, both in the manner in which power is distributed and in its administrative structure. When it comes to succession politics, a process more orderly than the hereditary feudal tradition of primogeniture will have to be developed in China. History has shown that the West can offer little to the non-Western world beyond rationalization of oppression and technologies of exploitation. If after four centuries of Western modernity the world is still beset with violence, hunger, exploitation and weapons of mass destruction on an unprecedented scale, it follows that its Mandate of Heaven is in jeopardy.

Chapter 5 - THE ABDUCTION OF MODERNITY Part 4: Taoism and Modernity

To know the Way,
We go the Way;
We do the Way
The way we do
The things we do.
It's all there in front of you,
But if you try too hard to see it,
You'll only become confused.

I am me,
And you are you,
As you can see;
But when you do,
The things you can do,
You will find the Way,
And the Way will follow you.

(The Tao of Pooh)

To Taoists, modernity is a meaningless concept because truth is timeless and life goes in circles. In post-modern thinking in the West, much of the awareness that Taoists have entertained for centuries is just now surfacing. Even in military strategy, Sun Tzu's *On the Art of War (Sunzi Bingfa)*, an ancient Taoist military treatise (500 BC), is now much in vogue in this modern age of weapons of mass destruction and remote-controlled precision bombs.

Historians are uncertain of the historical facts regarding Laozi, founder of Taoism. The name itself casts doubt on

Laozi's identity. *Ad verbum,* it simply means "old sage". Colloquially, the term *laozi* in modern Chinese has come to mean an arrogant version of "yours truly". The earliest documented information on Laozi appears in the classic *Records of the Historian (Shi Ji),* written by historian Sima Qian in 108 BC during the Han dynasty (206 BC-AD 220). It describes Laozi as a person named Li Er (born around 604 BC) who worked as a librarian in the court of the State of Eastern Zhou (Dong Zhou) during the Spring and Autumn Period (Chunqiu, 770-481 BC).

Laozi was reported to have met only once the young Confucius (Kongfuzi, 551-479 BC), who was 53 years his junior. If intellectual exchanges took place at that celebrated meeting, Confucius had to be at least in his late 20s, thus placing Laozi in his 80s when the two sages purportedly met. Confucius did not become widely known until 500 BC at the age of 51, which would put Laozi's age at 104 if they met as two intellectual celebrities. No wonder the pundit was called "old sage".

Laozi is generally accepted as author of the *Classic of the Virtuous Path (Daode Jing),* although evidence has been uncovered to suggest that it was actually written by others long after his time, albeit based on ideas ascribed to him. The *Book of Virtuous Path* is written in a style that is both cryptic and enigmatic. The true meanings of its messages are difficult to elucidate definitively. Its main attraction lies in the requirement of active reader participation for receiving the full benefit of its mystic insights. Each reading solicits new levels of insights from the reader depending on his or her experience, mood, mental alertness and preoccupation. It asks questions rather than provides answers. It is a book of revelation with an effect similar to what the Bible has on devoted Christians.

Zhuangzhou, a Zhou Dynasty skeptic and mystic who lived in 4th century BC, in his classic *Zhuangzi* expounded on many of Laozi's doctrines with original insight, ingenious construct, incisive witticism and delightful charm. Drawing on Taoist concepts, Zhuangzhou opposed and ridiculed the moral utilitarianism of Confucius.

Tao or Dao, a Chinese word meaning "way" or "path", delineates an enlightened perception of the mysterious ways of life. The path of life is revealed professedly only through spontaneous insights and creative breakthroughs. The alternating, self-renewing and circular phenomenon of nature such as day following night following day is an illuminating Taoist paradigm. The life-regenerating cycle of the seasons is another example. Taoists believe all in life to be inseparably interrelated. Taoists consider conventional wisdom illusionary. They point out that concepts are merely cognitive extremes of a consciousness continuum. Extremes exist only as contrasting points to give distinctive meanings to the unthinking, but in truth, these extremes are inseparable interdependent polarities. There can be no life without death, no goodness without evil and no happiness without tragedy. Light shines only in darkness. We only know something has been forgotten after we remember it. There is no modernity without tradition. Behind this dualistic illusion, a unifying, primary principle of life endures. It is called Tao.

To Taoists, the essence of life can be appreciated by observing the flow of water. The word "alive" *(huo)* in the Chinese language is composed of the root sign representing "water" *(shui)* and the modifying sign representing "tongue" *(she),* suggesting that flowing speech is the essence of living. Water, that fluid substance with no shape of its own, is capable of assuming the most intricate shapes of its containers. Any substance with a rigid form becomes prisoner to that form, unable to adapt to changing surroundings. Humans, whose lives are subject to infinite constraints, should attempt to adopt the flexibility of water to accommodate the intricate dimensions of the containers of life. Water, always taking the path of least resistance and most natural flow, seeking rest at the lowest point, preserving a level surface over irregular bottoms, overcoming stubborn obstacles, smoothing rough surfaces and rounding sharp edges of hard materials, provides a Taoist model for an enlightened man's approach to life's imperfections. In moderate amounts, water is a life-giving substance. In excessive amounts, it can be cataclysmic and it can drown life. Like water, life reacts violently and becomes destructive when forced. It can be peaceful and good when guided gently.

According to Taoist precept, *roushu* (flexible method) is an approach to be preferred over violent confrontation, which tends to be self-defeating and counterproductive. Meditation and calm contemplation are the means to spiritual liberation. They are the true instruments to man's salvation from obsessive fixations and from illusionary and distracting agitations of the physical senses. To attain without effort is nature's way. To attain with forced effort is an unenlightened man's folly, which will always be self-defeating. Judo, the Japanese art of physical combat that seeks to turn the opponent's own strength against himself, is derived from a Tang Taoist fighting style called *roushu.* The US "war on terror" has yet to understand the effectiveness of *roushu,* and until it does, it will remain self-defeating. Force produces counterforce. The use of fear as a deterrence operates like a concentric mirror, reflecting fear back on the point of initial radiation.

Every action reduces the range of one's options. Not taking premature or unnecessary actions keeps all of one's options open, so that the most appropriate action remains available. Actions always elicit reactions. Each action taken provokes reactions from all quarters that, taken together, are always more powerful than the precipitous action itself. It is the ultimate definition of the inescapable law of unintended consequences.

To follow the *dao* (path) of life is to go with the natural flow of life and to avoid going against it. The ethical theories of Taoism lean toward passive resistance, believing that evil, by definition, will ultimately destroy even itself without undue interference.

Yet it would be a mistake to regard Taoism as fatalistic and pessimistic, instead of the ultimate sophistication in optimism that it is. Controlled quantities of the bad can be good. Excessive amounts of the good can be bad. Poison kills. But when handled properly, it can cure diseases. Without poison, there can be no medicine. To employ poison to attack poison is a Taoist principle, which is validated in the modern medical practice of vaccination, the use of antibiotics and chemotherapy treatments.

Only by not applying effort can one achieve that state in which nothing is not attainable effortlessly *(wu-wei ze wu-suo-bu-wei)*. Every Taoist knows this famous Taoist assertion, although none can fully explain it. Translated, it reads literally: Only by avoiding effort can one achieve that state in which nothing is not attainable effortlessly. This well-known Taoist assertion, the inherent paradox of which defies logic, is still effortlessly driving modern students of Chinese philosophy insane.

A person's role in modern economic life, when observed with detached insight, illustrates the truth of the famous Taoist dilemma of aiming to be effortless.

Before one chooses a profession, one has the option of a wide range of endeavors with which to satisfy one's interest and to enable one to be useful in life. One can become a philosopher, an artist, a politician, a teacher, a scientist, a lawyer, a doctor, etc. As soon as one decides to be a lawyer, for example, then one can no longer afford to spend much time on other fields of endeavor, thus greatly narrowing one's options. If, in order to be the best in one's field, one devotes all of one's time and effort to the study of law and nothing else, one ends up being ignorant of other aspects of life. One can therefore end up aimlessly as a useless expert. Thus the exclusive study of law may neutralize one's original purpose, which is to lead a useful life by promoting justice. For a specialization to be truly useful, it needs to be defined so inclusively that excessive specialization itself becomes a pitfall to avoid. The corollary: the desire for one's objective will block one's attainment of it. This is so because the distracting impact of one's desire will obscure one's focus on the objective itself.

It is better not to act unless and until one is certain such action will not foreclose other options, rendering one paralyzed. But fear of action is paralysis itself. Unenlightened persons seek fame and fortune to achieve happiness, only to find that through obsessive seeking of fame and fortune, they destroy the very chance for happiness. They mistakenly regard fame and fortune, superficial trappings of happiness, as happiness itself. They slave after fame and fortune without realizing that it is that very slavery that will rob them of their happiness. Incidentally, "happiness" in the Chinese language is expressed by the term *kuai-huo,* which literally means "fast-living".

It is a Taoist axiom that intellectual scholarship and analytical logic can only serve to dissect and categorize information. Knowledge, different from information, is achieved only through knowing. Ultimately, only intuitive understanding can provide wisdom. Truth, while elusive, exists. But it is obscured by search, because purposeful search will inevitably mislead the searcher from truth. By focusing on the purpose, the searcher can only find what he is looking for.

How does one know what questions to ask about truth if one does not know what the elusive answers should be? Conversely, if one knows already what the answers should be, why does one need to ask questions? Lewis Carroll's Alice in *Alice's Adventures in Wonderland* (1865) would unknowingly be a Taoist.

Taoists believe that the *dao* (path) of life, since it eludes taxonomic definition and intellectual pursuit, can only be intuitively experienced through mystic meditation, by special breathing exercises and sexual techniques to enhance the mind and harmonize the body. They believe that these mind-purifying undertakings, coupled with an ascetic lifestyle and lean diet, would also serve to prolong life. Taoist philosophy is referred to as *Xuanxue,* literally "mystic learning".

Taoists consider the duty of a ruler to be that of protecting with minimal interference his subjects from harm, often from themselves, thus avoiding the overriding injury that excessive intervention would bring. A truly wise ruler should act in the way nature's unseen hand gently protects the good, the definition of which is complex and philosophical. The word "governance" *(zhi)* in Chinese is composed of the root sign of "water" *(shui)* and the modifying sign of "platform" *(tai),* suggesting that to govern is similar to preserving stability of a floating platform on water. Excessive and unbalanced interference, even when motivated by good intention, does not always produce good results. Periodic, mild famines may be considered good in the long run because the people will learn lessons from them on the need for grain storage. Excessive prosperity may be considered bad because it leads to wasteful consumption with environmental and spiritual pollution that eventually will destroy the good life. Present-day economists would come to appreciate the desirability of sustainable balanced moderate economic growth over the alternative of fluctuating booms and busts.

Taoists consider Confucian reliance on the Code of Rites (Liji) to guide socio-political behavior as oppressive and self-defeating. The Code of Rites is the ritual compendium as defined by Confucius to prescribe proper individual behavior in a hierarchical society. Taoists regard blind Confucian penchant for moralistic coercion as misguided. Such coercion neglects the true power of *roushu* (flexible method). Taoists think that ultimately, great success always leads to great failure because each successful stage makes the next stage more difficult until, by definition, failure inevitably results. To Taoists, the assertion that nothing succeeds like success is false. In truth, nothing fails like success. Success is always the root of future failure.

Since the only way to avoid the trap of life's vicious circle is to limit one's ambition, why not eliminate ambition entirely? Would that not ensure success in life? But a little ambition is a good thing. Total elimination, even of undesirables, is an extreme solution, and it is therefore self-defeating. Besides, the paradox is that eliminating all goals is itself a goal, thus guaranteeing built-in failure. An example of this is the futility of a compulsive organizer who makes a list of ways to relax. From the traveler's point of view, no matter how many times he changes direction, he always ends up where he is heading. Life is a prison from which one can escape only if one does not try to escape. It is the desire to escape that makes a place a prison, and the desire to return that makes it a home. Home is not where one is; it is where one wants to return.

Taoism as religion is generally regarded by intellectuals as a corruption of its essence as philosophy. Having evolved originally from a mystic search for truth, Taoism has gradually degenerated into practices of secular alchemy aiming to achieve the transformation of commonplace metals into gold, and to discover cures for diseases and formulae for longevity and secrets to immortality.

The historical justification for this censorious view of Taoism as religion gone awry comes from Taoist movements such as the Yellow Turbans Disturbance (Huangjin Huo). It is so labeled by the contemptuous Confucian establishment. Beginning around AD 170, shortly before the final collapse of the Han Dynasty (206 BC-AD 220), roaming bands of disaffected peasants mounted a decade-long disruption of the peace in the provinces. Eventually, in AD 184, exploiting aggravating dislocations caused by floods along lower Yellow River (Huanghe), a messianic mass movement of social revolution developed in areas between modern-day Shandong and Henan provinces.

Historians call the movement the Yellow Turbans Peasant Rebellion (Huangjin Minbian) because its peasant members identified themselves by wearing yellow turbans around their heads. It was the first major peasant revolt in Chinese history. The leader of the rebellion was Zhang Jiao, chief patriarch of the Taoist sect of the Way of Celestial Peace (Taiping Dao). Zhang Jiao had been an unsuccessful candidate in *keju* (public examinations) for officialdom. While gathering herbal medicine in the mountainous wilderness, he allegedly met an old sage named the South China Ancient Sage (Nanhua Laoxian) from whom he received the three-volume *Celestial Peace Methods (Taiping Yaoshe)*. A talented propagandist and messianic faith-healer, Zhang Jiao proclaimed himself pope of a new religion based on a synthesis of Huangdi (Yellow Emperor), primeval mythical sovereign, and a deified Laozi, founder of Taoism.

125

Huangdi is the ritual appellation adopted by the first monarch in Chinese history, a man named Gongsun, allegedly born on the celestial star Xuanyuan. Legend has it that Huangdi established the first kingdom in history at Youxiong, around Zhengzhou in modern-day Henan province. During his reign, language, costume, architecture, money, measure, medicine and music were professedly invented.

All Chinese consider themselves descendants of Huangdi. *Huang* (yellow) is the color of ripe wheat. The concept of "yellow" commands a mythical meaning in Chinese culture, signifying regality, prosperity and civilization, all symbolized by the color of golden harvest.

The Yellow Turbans, with a theocratic organization of more than 500,000 zealous cadres leading an army of 360,000 at the height of its influence in AD 184, were ruled with supreme power by Zhang Jiao and his two brothers. The three brothers, as the Trinity of Lords of Heaven, Earth and Men respectively, were supported by a hierarchy of militarized clergy. Communal living was

126

practiced with regular public confessions, mass participation in spiritual trances and orgiastic ceremonies in which men and women engaged in prolonged kisses to "balance their vital vapor (*luoji*)". Diseases were considered consequences of sin and were believed to be curable by healing amulets applied to affected parts of the body and therapeutic charms worn around the neck or waist.

The Yellow Turbans Rebellion was finally suppressed by renegade army commanders of the falling Han Dynasty who became independent warlords and who kept China fragmented for three more centuries, after AD 220, before Yang Jian reunited the country by founding the Sui Dynasty in 581.

Near Luoyang, 65 kilometers southeast, in Songshan, epicenter of Chinese Buddhist geo-cosmology, is situated the legendary Shaolin Si (Young Forest Temple). Shaolin Si (aka Shaolin Temple) is the birthplace of Chan Buddhism and the epic cradle of Chinese martial arts. The warring skills of the *sengs* of Shaolin Si have been famous since the 4th century AD. Even in modern times, tourists from the world over flock to this monastery to visit this center of *wushu,* the martial art known popularly as *gongfu* (commonly referred to in English as "kung fu"). Shaolinquan (Shaolin-style Boxing) is the illustrious style of martial arts that traces its origin to Shaolin Si at the time of its founding. Shaolin Si was founded by an Indian prince of Persian-Samarkand roots named Boddhidharma (Da'mo in Chinese) during the Bei Wei Dynasty (Northern Wei, 386-534) in the 4th century. Boddhidharma was the founder of a sect *(zong)* of

Buddhism known as Chan, later known as Zen Buddhism in Japan and the West.

Chan is a Chinese transfiguration of the Sanskrit word *dhyana,* meaning "contemplation for truth", while Zen is its Japanese pronunciation and Yoga is its equivalent in Sanskrit. Chan precepts assert that intellectual effort, good work, performance of rituals and other traditional Buddhist practices are not only of little inherent merit but also are often hindrances to the quest for true insight into the enlightened meaning of reality. Spiritual salvation can only be found by introspective inquiries into one's inner soul. Purity surpasses all.

After its import to China from India, Chan Buddhism in Tang China derived an anti-scholastic, anti-textual and anti-exegetical bias from the mystic teachings of Taoism *(Dao Jia xuanxue).*

Shortly after his death, Boddhidharma was reportedly seen in person at Mount Cong (Congling) of Songshan by Song Yun, an official of the court of Bei Wei. The disciples of Bodhidharma excavated their master's grave after the miraculous incident, only to find his discarded burial clothes *sans* body. Something similar happened to a man named Jesus. Ascension to heaven for the pure of soul while alive is an ancient notion in Taoist concepts, although ascension after death is more a Christian notion than a Taoist one. The Virgin Mary is declared by Pope Pius XII's 1950 bull *Munificentissimus Deus,* as an article of faith, to have been "assumed" directly into heaven in the body. Imperial Prince Jin, a Taoist holy prince, the pious son of Emperor Lin of the ancient Zhou Dynasty (1027-256 BC) who ruled from 571-546 BC, was reported to have ascended to heaven before death, riding a white crane.

Chan (Zen) teaching stresses spontaneous oral instructions, Socratic in style, through the use of mystical paradoxes to reach beyond the rigid limits of deductive logic. It also derives from Taoist mystical teaching a love of nature and a preference for the rustic, ascetic life. Simplicity and purity are the highest goals of Chan spiritual attainment. The key concept in Chan philosophy is *xu* (void). Voidness is the fullest attainment from existence. Nothingness is all and all is nothingness: the ultimate nihilism.

Chan Buddhism in time split into the Northern and Southern sects, headed respectively by Chenxiu and Hui'neng. Chenxiu and Hui'neng were both disciples of

129

the late Master Hongren, the fifth patriarch after the founder of Chan Buddhism, Boddhidharma (Da'mo) of Songshan. When quizzed by the late Master Hongren at his deathbed, in a test to select the master's successor, about the extent of their respective enlightenment, Chenxiu, the master's protege, proclaimed that his enlightenment was comparable to the sacred banyan tree and his heart was as calm as an alter mirror. To his fellow monk's flowery assertion of having attained an immaculate state of *xu*, Hui'neng dispassionately proclaimed the famous counter-remark: "Fundamentally, there is no significance in the banyan tree; and there is no magic in a mirror. To be truly enlightened, these material things ought to have no meaning."

After the death of Master Hongren in 647, Chenxiu went south to Jingzhou, in modern-day Hubei province, leaving their master's legacy at Xiaolin Si in Songshan to his more enlightened fellow *seng* (Buddhist monk). But Hui'neng, in keeping with true enlightenment, elected to retire farther south with his counter-culture sect to Shaozhou, in modern-day Hunan province, to shun the undesirable pollution of unsolicited celebrity, thus becoming known as the Southern Sect (Nanzong). Headed by Chenxiu, the Northern Sect (Beizong), so named because Hui'neng's sect had gone farther south, placed emphasis on teachings and gradual, incremental enlightenment.

By contrast, the Southern Sect, headed by Hui'neng, places emphasis on inspiration rather than teaching, and emphasizes insightful flashes in place of gradual understanding for attaining enlightenment. The Southern

130

Sect spread widely in subsequent centuries without organized evangelism.

After Hui'neng, master of the Southern Sect (Nanzong), settled at Shao Mountain in Shaozhou, legend has it that all the wild tigers and leopards, which previously had roamed the wilderness and menaced the nearby population, miraculously disappeared, causing his reputation of holiness to spread. Modern-day wildlife preservationists would not have found Hui'neng's achievements admirable.

Chenxiu repeatedly invited Hui'neng to court, but the Master of the Southern Sect, true to his Chan (Zen) principles, declined each time. Chenxiu finally wrote personally to Hui'neng to implore him to come to court, but Hui'neng continued to decline steadfastly and is reported to have said dispassionately to the messenger sent by Chenxiu: "My form is ugly. When the northern soil sees it, I am afraid no respect for my methods would be forthcoming. Besides, my master felt that the Southern Sect and I are of the same destiny. It should be not altered." Hui'neng died without ever going north.

The Southern Sect of Hui'neng flourished in succeeding centuries while the Northern Sect of Chenxiu, despite imperial sponsorship, withered into a minor, esoteric cult. The history of these two sects illustrates that glory is ephemeral while enlightenment endures.

Hui'neng's Southern Sect was later divided into Qingyuan (Pure Spring) and Nanyue (South Mount) movements. The Qingyuan movement evolved into three branches,

Cao'dong (Cave of Cao), Yunmen (Gate of Cloud) and Fayan (Method's Eye). The Nanyue movement further evolved into two branches: Linji (Reach Charity) and Weiyang (Active Respect).

Chan (Zen) Buddhism was introduced to Japan by Japanese monks who had visited China, particularly Eisai (1141-1215), who brought back the Linji sect (Rinzai in Japanese) in 1191, and his disciple Dogen (1200-53), who imported the Cao'dong sect (Soto in Japanese) in 1277.

In Japan, Zen emphasis on personal character and discipline, combined with commitment on worldly activism, became the spiritual ideals of the medieval Samurai class. Zen monasteries such as those in Kyoto and Kamakura became religious, intellectual and artistic centers. Zen Buddhism was suppressed in Japan after the Meiji Restoration (1867-68), when nationalistic Shinto religious movements were officially encouraged. Nevertheless, Zen Buddhism remains the most popular Buddhist sect in Japan today.

US General Douglas MacArthur compelled Japanese

Emperor Hirohito to disavow divinity in the historic 1946 New Year rescript, temporarily dismantling the fundamental foundation of state Shintoism. The deification traditionally implied in the title of Heaven Emperor (Tianhuang), in use since the 7th century by all Japanese monarchs, and the same title originally used by the High Heritage Emperor (Gaozong) of the Tang Dynasty of China, is now forsaken, though the use of the title itself is preserved. To many traditional Japanese, despite intellectual disavowal, the Heaven Emperor is still a godly figure, as the title literally suggests.

MacArthur also forbade occupied Japan to use public funds for the support of state Shintoism, which had been identified with Japanese militarism. In less than a decade after the defeat of Japan by the Allies, Shintoism experienced a revival in Japan, particularly in right-wing politics, while Rinzai Zen (Linji Chan in Chinese) gained considerable following in the United States after World War II, largely because of the devotion of returning Americans favorably exposed to the ascetic sect.

Chan Buddhism became influential in China only after the 10th century, together with the other popular Buddhist movement known as the Pure Land (Jingtu) sect, which practiced the invocation of the name of Amita Buddha (Amituofo) as an expression of the acceptance of fate and the rejection of futile secular anxiety. Amita Buddha (Amituofo) was the supreme master of a class of Mahayana deities who supposedly resided in the Western Paradise known as Jingtu (Pure Land).

Along with other Mahayana sects, the Jingtu sect believed that any individual, if he or she devoted his or her life to doing good, could become a Boddhisattva, a deity worshipped in Mahayana Buddhism who, having achieved enlightenment, compassionately refrains from entering nirvana in order to save others.

However, the Jingtu sect, with branches named Shandao (Good Way, Jodo in Japanese) and Ci'min (Merciful Union, Shin in Japanese), promised a heavenly salvation in Jingtu, the Western Paradise of Amita Buddha, for the devotee of unshakable faith, which supersedes good works in importance.

The true believer could even eat meat, indulge in sexual pleasure and maintain secular families without compromising his holiness, a practice condoned by the Japanese Shin sect for its priests in modern times.

While in its most vigorous form, Jingtu Buddhism encompasses the ultra-sophistication of the Taoist concept of the necessary function of temptation, the absence of which negates the possibility of virtue; it is also a concept most vulnerable to unprincipled abuse by those less than vigorous in piety and by outright charlatans.

For while the ordeal of temptation may provide the opportunity to manifest commitment to holiness, the surrender to temptation itself cannot be proof of having achieved holiness.

Feodor Dostoyevsky (1812-81) asserted in a fearful warning: "If God does not exist, everything is permitted." To that, Jingtu Buddhists would respond: "Only if God exists everything is permitted." Voltaire was right when he said that if God does not exist, man (both Dostoyevsky and the Jingtu Buddhists) would have to invent him. The atheists' denial of the existence of God, maintained with equal disregard for rationality as their believer opponents, is not as dangerous as their corollary claim of God's irrelevance. Atheists would suffer the penalty of being the sure loser of Pascal's wager.

Blaise Pascal (1632-62), French mathematician, scientist, founder of the theory of probability, and religious philosopher, was an anti-Jesuit Jansenite who, following Antoine Arnauld of the Sorbonne, ran afoul of the Church for his controversial predestinarianism. Pascal argued that while the inadequacy of reason cannot resolve questions of divinity, it is safer to bet on the possibility of the existence of God, because the penalty for error would be minor and the reward of being right would be infinite. Believing in a non-existent God would do us no harm, and believing in an existent God would grant us the grace of heaven. Conversely, denying a non-existing God would win us nothing, while denying an existent God would land us in hell. Pascal offered the world a perfect hedge.

One could argue, however, that believing in something not true is not harmless, and God, being omnipotent and all-knowing, would sympathize with an intelligent man's honest obligation to reject blind faith, and would discount a calculating faith based on opportunism. So a Cartesian doubt appears an intelligent option for an unknowable question. It led Rene Descartes (1596-1650) to his famous conclusion, *cogito ergo sum* (I think, therefore I am), which proves the existence of the thinking mind but leaves the question of God not satisfactorily answered. Descartes inverted claim made three centuries earlier by Thomas Aquinas that the experience of God is implied by the general facts of the universe, by claiming that these facts could not be known without a knowledge of God.

The less-than-satisfactory assertions of both Aquinas and Descartes issued an invitation two centuries later to agnosticism, a term coined by Thomas Henry Huxley (1825-95), English biologist and educator. Aspects of agnosticism are in fact classic Taoist prepositions, certainly the parts concerning doubts, if not the parts placing faith in rational inquiry and scientific methods. Thomas Huxley, grandfather of Aldous Huxley (1894-1963) of *Brave New World* fame, doubted all things not immediately open to logical analysis and scientific verification, and held up truth as an ideal state, scientific methods as the tools of truth and evolution as the fruit of truth. Ironically, Aldous, the grandson of Thomas, after

three generations of conspicuous Huxleyan scientific
piety, wrote an earth-shaking novel on the horrors and
futility of scientific progress. The Taoist notion of life
going in full circles is once again demonstrated in the
Huxley saga. Confucian scholars throughout the ages
remained ambivalent toward Chan Buddhism. Liu
Zongyuan (773-819), the neo-Confucian author of a
classic apology for feudalism titled *Discourse on
Feudalism (Fengjian Lun)*, composed a famous poem
titled "Studying Chan Sutra" *(Du Chan Jing)*, expressing
his skepticism of Chan mysticism and his admiration for
Taoist enlightenment (inadequately translated by this
writer):

Drawing from a well to rinse cold chattering teeth,
With a pure heart casting off secular trappings;
Leisurely holding the Buddhist sutra,
Pacing from the east den while studying.

The fundamental truth not being understood,
Absurd claims become society's pursuits;
Wishing for depth from past writing,
Can nature be affected by memorizing?

The garden of the Taoist is placid,
Green moss links verdant bamboo;
The sun pierces through the morning mist,
The green firs appear coated with ointment,
Insipidly hard to verbalize,
Sanguine perception replenishes a heart self
gratified.

Taoist enlightenment is the diametrical opposite of the

West's notion of enlightenment as presented during the Age of Reason, also known as the Age of Enlightenment, hailed by Western scholars as the root of modernity.

Chapter 6 - THE ABDUCTION OF MODERNITY Part 5: The Enlightenment & Modernity

The Enlightenment, generally accepted as the flowering of modernity in the West from its Renaissance roots, is a periodization in history. Periodization, a complex problem in history, is the attempt to categorize or divide historical time, mentality or events into discrete named blocks. History is in fact continuous, and so all systems of periodization are to some extent arbitrary. History does not end as long as the human species survives. Those who proclaim the end of history are predicting the death of civilization, not the victory of neo-liberalism as heaven on Earth. Imperialism and neo-imperialism, operating with cultural hegemony, are a cancer the invasive growth of which will kill the world as a living organism.

It is nevertheless useful to segment history so that the past can provide lessons to the present by being conceptually organized and significant changes over time articulated. Different peoples and cultures have different histories, and so will need different models of periodization. Periodizing labels constantly change and are subject to redefinition as contemporary perceptions change. A historian may claim that there is no such thing as modernity, or the Enlightenment or the Renaissance, or the Nuclear Age, while others will defend the concept. Modernity, as currently constituted in the West, can also be viewed as a relapse of civilization toward barbarism through advanced technology.

Many periodizing concepts apply only in specific conditions, but they are often mistaken as universal generalities. Some have a cultural usage (such the Romantic period, the Age of Reason or the Age of Science or the Space Age), others refer to historical events (the Age of Imperialism, the Depression Years or the New Deal era) and others are defined by decimal numbering systems (the 1960s, the 16th century).

In chronology, an era is a period reckoned from an artificially fixed point in time, as before or after the birth of Christ: BC for Before Christ and AD for Anno Domini (year of the Lord). There are less known but also significant points in historical time beside the birth of Christ. The alleged creation of the world in Jewish mythical history is equivalent to 3761 BC, and in Byzantine history, the creation date was 5508 BC. The founding of the city of Rome took place in 753 BC, with subsequent years marked AUD for *ad urbe condita* (from the founding of the city). The *hijira* marks the migration of the Prophet Mohammed to Medina from Mecca in AD 622. Abbreviated AH, it is the starting timepost for all Muslims.

The division between AD and BC defines history according to the birth of one man, whose divinity is far from universally accepted. Only about 33 percent of the world's population is Christians. The most far-reaching date anomaly is the late setting of the beginning of the Christian era by the Roman monk-scholar Dionysius Exiguous (died circa AD 545), thus putting the historical birth of Christ at 4 BC, four years before the calendar birth year of Christ. The year AD 2000 marks two chronological events in the Western calendar: a new millennium and a new century. Its celebration marks the global dominance of Western culture in the 20th century. The new millennium is merely year 4398 in Chinese lunar calendar - a non-event.

The French revolutionary calendar changed the names of the months to remove all reminders of despotic traditions, such as August, named after the Roman emperor Augustus, July, named after Julius Caesar, and March (*mars* in French), named after the Roman god of war. It made all months 30 days equally to emphasize equality and rationality. The names for the months in the new calendar were invented hastily, by revolutionary dramatist Philippe Fabre d'Eglantine (1755-94), George Jacques Danton's talented secretary who would be tragically guillotined at the prime age of 39, a mere five years after the storming of the Bastille, the popular uprising that launched the French Revolution. The 12 30-day months added up to 360 days; the remaining five days of the year, called *sans-culottides,* after the name given to the members of the lower classes not wearing fancy *culottes* (breeches), were to be feast days for the

141

laboring class, called Virtue, Genius, Labor, Reason and Rewards.

The French revolutionary calendar rejected the year of the birth of Christ as the first Anno Domini. It replaced the seven-day week, viewed by revolutionary zealots as an obsolete Christian relic, with the metric 10-day decade, unwittingly causing a counterrevolutionary, regressive reduction in the number of days of rest for the working populace from four to three in a month. The overall purpose was to remove from the cultural consciousness all Christian events such as Christmas, Easter, All Saints Day, the Sabbath, etc, as part of a program to replace Christianity with a Cult of Reason. The French revolutionary calendar remained in effect until the Thermidorian Reaction, a period of political revisionism, of vulgar extravagance in social manners, of greed and scandal and of *merveilleuses,* women known for their underdressed overdressing in public. The Thermidorian Reaction was marked by the growth of corruption, inflationary speculation and manipulative profiteering, suspension of populist economic regulations, topped with a wholesale repeal of de-Christianization practices.

The Thermidorian Reaction is so named because it came after the coup d'etat of 9 Thermidor, Year III of the Republic (July 27, 1794), that brought down Maximilien Robespierre (1758-94), thus ending the Reign of Terror, and brought to power a convenient coalition of the conservative old bourgeoisie and the boisterous *parvenus* and *nouveaux riches,* which would deliver the French nation, another five years later, to a military dictator in the person of Napoleon Bonaparte.

Still other periodizations are derived from influential or talismanic individuals (the Victorian era, the Elizabethan era, the Napoleonic era or the Mao era). Some of these usages are geographically specific. This is especially true of periodizing labels derived from individuals or ruling elites, such as the Jacksonian era in the United States, or the Meiji era in Japan, or the Merovingian period in France. Cultural terms may also have a limited reach. Thus the concept of the Romantic period may be meaningless outside of Europe and of Europe-influenced cultures.

Yet the term "modernity" takes on universal

143

characteristics that spring from Western cultural hegemony. In recent times, modernity has again been abducted as a war cry to perpetuate the domination by the capitalist West of the rest of the world. Previously, the Renaissance claimed modernity as a justification against secular power of the Church, the bourgeoisie claimed modernity as a justification against absolute monarchism, and the socialist revolutions claimed modernity as justification against capitalism. All these claims were associated with social progress. But the current abduction of modernity by the capitalistic West represents the first time in history when reaction is claimed as modernity and barbarism as progress. The law of the jungle is celebrated as competitive market fundamentalism, and the doctrine of "might is right" permeates modern diplomacy, replacing morality and legitimacy.

Periodizing terms are often tools of cultural hegemony with negative connotation for oppressed cultures and positive connotation for the hegemonic culture. Thus there is the Age of Monarchy in the West but the Age of Asiatic and Oriental Tyrants in Asia and the Middle East. The Victorian era, which is known for sexual repression, racism, class conflict and exploitation, and imperialism, is hailed in the West as the age of propriety, industrialization and capitalism. Other labels such as "Renaissance" have positive characteristics as compared with "Medieval", despite that fact that historians have suggested that unlike the Middle Ages, the Renaissance failed to develop significant lasting social institutions.

renaissance

The French term "Renaissance" - meaning "rebirth" though in the English-speaking world it is commonly known by its French name - was created by Petrarch (Francesco Petrarca, 1304-74), an Italian humanist poet whose famous vernacular poem inspired by his love for Laura transcended medieval asceticism into individual expression of emotion. The term refers to the cultural changes that occurred in Italy as a reaction to Italian conditions of the time, which began around the *quattrocento* (15th century) and culminated in what is termed the High Renaissance, at around 1500. Many Western historians regard the Renaissance as the beginning of modernity. Yet, the basic institutions, the great framework of collective purpose and action by which the West continues to operate far into the present time, all originated in the Middle Ages. Parliaments, for example, were medieval feudal institutions. The Magna Carta was signed by King John of England in 1215.

The Renaissance, also known as the Age of Humanism, was a period of secularization of Western civilization. The Renaissance Church became a secular institution in this period, shedding its spiritual roots, with insatiable greed for material wealth and temporal power. The Italian

Renaissance produced little of what could be considered great ideas or institutions by which men living in society could be held together in harmony. Indeed, the greatest of all Europeans institutions, the Roman Church, in which Europeans had lived for centuries, fell into neglect under Renaissance popes, whose fall from spiritual grace sparked the Reformation.

Nor did the Renaissance produce any effectual political institutions. Unlike the medieval agricultural towns of France that developed gradually, the trading towns of Italy prospered abruptly as trade converged on the Mediterranean. The sudden riches from trade held in private hands required a new culture separate from the medieval communal spirit to rationalize its acceptability. As merchants made obscene fortunes from trade and banking, they diverted social criticism by sponsoring art, to glorify their worldly sins with beauty. Successful bankers lent money to popes, kings and princes, and with the profits they gained political control of Italian trading towns to turn them into despotic city-states. They employed mercenaries in the form of *condottieri,* private captains of armed bands, who contracted with opposing city-states to carry on warfare, sometime even changing sides during hostility for a better price. As they forgot about things that money could not buy, they glorified the power of money in a philosophy of humanism and despotism.

The most notable example was the Medici clan of Florence. Giovanni (died 1429) founded the banking fortune that enabled his son Cosimo de' Medici (1389-1464) to become the de facto ruler of Florence through populist politics. Cosimo's grandson, Lorenzo the Magnificent (1449-92), used his great wealth to govern as a connoisseur and lavish benefactor of art and letters. Tuscany became a duchy of which Medici men were hereditary grand dukes until the clan died out in 1753. The clan furnished two popes and numerous cardinals to the Church, and two Medici women became queens of France. It was the first time in history when money led to political significance rather than the reverse. Italian politics degenerated into a tangled web of subterfuge and conspiracy, making no pretense to legitimacy, to represent any moral idea or to further any social good.

The Renaissance idea of *virtu* (to be man) had little to do with the medieval idea of virtue. *Virtu* describes the quality of being a man in the sense of demonstrating individual human powers as expressed in the arts, in war and statecraft. It is the root of Friedrich Wilhelm Nietzsche's hero and the rationale of fascism. This concept applies dominantly to the visual arts, referring to the work of Michelangelo, Raphael and Leonardo da Vinci. It also applies to the emergence of capitalism, private banking, provincial despotism and materialistic secularism. It celebrated the specific differences in man in contrast to the medieval concept of the common generality of man. The discovery of the rules of perspective and detailed anatomy in drawing allowed painters to locate humanity in specific contexts rather than symbolic generality of abstract truth. In Leonardo's *The Last Supper,* Christ and his disciples were portrayed as a group of men each having distinct individual personalities.

The Renaissance was a movement of the non-aristocratic elite minority, exclusive in spirit in contrast to the medieval notion of community. Renaissance individualism was the privilege of a dazzling few. The Italian humanists were lay writers, instead of clerics or court scribes. "Humanism" is a name given to the literary movement of the Italian Renaissance. The pomposity of the humanists was mocked by the populace in their own time. The humanists were in awe of antiquity, a peculiar preoccupation for modernists. They tried to dress, talk, and comport themselves like Roman nobles. They disdained writing in Italian as Dante Alighieri and Giovanni Boccaccio had done. They dismissed even medieval Latin as barbaric and corrupt, and reverted to the style of the excessively flowery language of the schoolbook Latin of Cicero (106-43 BC), the great Roman orator whose famous *First Oration Against Catiline* skillfully condemned Catiline as a conspirator based on hearsay testimony obtained from Catiline's mistress. Cicero, despite his rhetorical eloquence, remained unable to substantiate his legal authority to execute Catiline's five associates, thus subjecting himself to exile subsequently for having put to death Roman citizens without due process of law.

The Humanist movement did not survive the test of time, the exception being Lorenzo Valla (1407-57), who showed conclusively from the language used in the document that the Donation of Constantine, on which the papacy based it temporal claims, could not have been written in Constantine's time and so was a forgery. The discovery was welcomed by the Italian Renaissance city-state despots who were eager to undermine the legitimacy of the papacy's temporal power.

The Renaissance invented the idea of the "gentleman", later emulated by the British elite. Baldassare Castiglione (1478-1520) wrote *Book of the Courtier,* liberating Europeans from their uncouth manners of publicly spitting, belching, blowing their noses on their sleeves, snatching food with their bare hands and general bawling and sulking openly with little inhibition. According to Castiglione, a courtier should cultivate graceful manners in society and poised approaches toward his equals, converse with facility, be proficient in sports and arms, be an expert dancer with appreciation for music and poetry and be gallant to the fair sex. He should know Latin and Greek as a sign of good education and be familiar with literary trends but not too engrossed. In sum, it was a promotion of dilettantism, which as transformed into the English gentleman of the Oxbridge variety became what many identified as the mentality that contributed to the demise of the British Empire. It was also the mentality of much of the British-trained Third World elite. This mentality left the post-colonial independent nations with a poverty of political and economic leadership after the fall of the British Empire, from India to the Middle East, from Africa to Asia. Such mentality has kept the former colonies from cultural and economic revitalization from the wounds of colonialism.

Niccolo Machiavelli's *The Prince* (1513) was Europe's first secular treatise on politics, devoid of concern for morality, legitimacy or justice, issues that rulers have since learned to manipulate to rationalize their political interests. He described the barbaric chaos of 16th-century

Italy as universal modern reality. Ironically, this perspective deprived Italy of the development of institutions, such as the nation-state, in which men can act in concert for a larger purpose. In a new age of rising national monarchies, the city-states of Italy could not compete without the protection of the spiritual and temporal power of the Church, against which Renaissance Italy itself played a central role in weakening. In 1494, a French army crossed the Alps and Italy became the bone of contention between France and Spain. In 1527, a horde of undisciplined Spanish and German mercenaries sacked Rome, killing thousands in an orgy of rape and looting, imprisoned the pope and mockingly paraded cardinals facing backward on mules in the streets. Never had Rome experienced anything so horrible and degrading, not even from the barbaric Goths of the 5th century.

The term "Middle Ages" also derived from Petrarch, who was comparing his own period to the Ancient or Classical world, seeing his time as a time of rebirth after a dark intermediate period, the Middle Ages. The idea that the Middle Ages were a "middle" phase between two other large-scale periodizing concepts - Ancient and Modern - still persists. Smaller periodizing concepts such as Dark Ages occur within it. Both "Dark Ages" and "Middle Ages" still have negative connotations - the latter especially in its Latin form "medieval". However, other terms, such as "Gothic" as in Gothic architecture, used to refer to a style typical of the High Middle Ages, have largely lost the negative connotations they initially had, only to acquire others. Critics derisively called the French Physiocrats of the French Enlightenment "economists" because they concerned themselves with materialistic issues.

The Gothic and the Baroque were both named during subsequent stylistic periods when the preceding style had become unpopular. The word "Gothic" was applied as a pejorative term to all things Northern European and, hence, barbarian, by Italian writers during the 15th and 16th centuries. The word *baroque* was used first in late 18th century French to depict the irregular natural pearl shape and later an architectural style perceived to be boisterously irregular and larger than life, in comparison with the highly restrained regularity of Neoclassical architecture. Subsequently, these terms have become purely descriptive, and have largely lost negative connotations. However, the term "Baroque" as applied to art (for example Peter Paul Rubens) refers to a much earlier historical period than when applied to music (George Frideric Handel, Johann Sebastian Bach). This reflects the difference between stylistic histories internal to an art form and the external chronological history beyond it.

Gothic construction, most identifiable in popular culture by the flying buttress, is the technological response to the medieval pious aspiration toward light and height transformed into ecclesiastical architecture. The boisterous Baroque was the awe-inspiring instrument of the Counter-reformation, sponsored by the Jesuits, defenders of the True Faith. Baroque architecture was the propaganda vehicle of the Jesuits in their counter-reformation campaign and the dramatic stage of the Inquisition. It spread quickly to all Roman Catholic countries. King Louis XIV of France later coopted the propaganda effectiveness of the Baroque and the stately legitimacy of Classicism to enshrine the stature of absolute monarchy. Modern architecture rose from the hopes of social democratic ideals stemming from the collapse, in the aftermath of World War I, of the European monarchies and their attendant social and esthetic values as constituted in the system of court-sponsored academies. While the cultured public welcomed the new artistic philosophy, official suppression of the Modern Movement by both Nazi Germany and the post-Lenin Soviet Union forced its migration to the United States, where it was coopted into the service of corporate capitalism after being sanitized of most of its social-democratic program, the way modernity is now being abducted to serve the current "war on terrorism".

The entire Renaissance was supported by a political ideology that is of dubious acceptability by contemporary standards. Despotism was a boon to Italian Renaissance art and architecture. A case can be made to condemn the Italian Renaissance as a movement of courtly pretension and elitist taste prescribed by theme, content and form to the questionable needs of secular potentates and ecclesiastical mania. The noblest social art, one can argue, is that which the contribution of multitudes create for themselves as a common gift of glory, such as the Gothic cathedrals and the temples of ancient Greece. By contrast, Vladimir Tatlin's monument for the Third International was an attempt to unite artistic expression with the new socialist ideal as the Eiffel Tower did for industrialization. The Productivist Group maintained in

153

its polemic that material and intellectual production were of the same order. Leftist artists devoted their energy to making propaganda for the new Soviet government by painting the surfaces of all means of transport with revolutionary images to be viewed in remote corners of the collapsing czarist empire. Constructivism declared all-out war on bourgeois art. Alas, the revolutionary movement met its demise not from bourgeois resistance, but from internal doctrinal inquisition. Much of Constructivist esthetic creativity was subsequently coopted by bourgeois society. Modernity is socialism, but the term has been abducted by bourgeois capitalism since the end of the Cold War.

In many cases, those living through a period are unable to identify themselves as belonging to the "period" historians may later assign to them. This is partly because they are unable to predict the future, and so will not be able to tell whether they are at the beginning, middle or end of a period. Another reason may be that their own sense of historical development may be determined by religions or ideologies that differ from those used by later historians. We may well be living in the dawning of the age of socialism, free from the false starts of the past century, and ushered in finally by the self-destructive excesses of capitalism run amok.

It is important to recognize the difference between self-defined historical periods and those, which are later, defined by historians. At the beginning of the 20th century there was a general belief that culture, politics and history were entering a new era - that the new century would also be a new "era" in human

154

development. This belief in progress had been largely abandoned by the end of the century with the triumph of militant reaction crowned by a proclamation of the end of history. Yet just as the Catholic Counter-Reformation failed to arrest the spread of the Reformation, the capitalist reaction against the socialist revolutionary movement since 1848 is faced with the option of including socialist programs in the capitalist system or the replacement of capitalism by socialism. Democracy is not the exclusive tool of the bourgeoisie. Just as the bourgeoisie used democracy and the rebellious power of the working class to pressure the aristocracy, the working class will use democracy to remove the bourgeoisie from controlling the fate of the human race.

"The Enlightenment" is a periodization term that applies to the mainstream of thought of 18th century Europe. The scientific and intellectual developments of the 17th century fostered the belief in natural laws and universal order and the confidence in reason, which spread to influence 18th century society in Europe. These developments were typified by the discoveries of Isaac Newton (1642-1727), the rationalism of Rene Descartes (1596-1650) and Pierre Bayle (1647-1700), the pantheism of Baruch Spinoza (1632-77) that equates god with the forces and natural laws of the universe and the empiricism of Francis Bacon (1561-1626) and John Locke (1632-1704). A rational and scientific approach to religious, social, political and economic issues promoted a secular view of the world and a general sense of progress and perfectibility. **I am amazed that Liu fails to mention here that the Christian Reformation sparked by Martin Luther's nailing his 95 Theses on**

the church door at Wittenberg, had a purifying effect on the Christian church and brought back spirituality and true bible doctrine.

The proponents of the Enlightenment were of one mind on certain basic attitudes, and sought to discover and act on universally valid principles governing humanity, nature and society. They attacked spiritual and scientific authority, dogmatism, intolerance, censorship and economic and social constraints. They considered the state the proper and rational instrument of progress. In England, Lockean theories of learning by sense perception were carried forward by David Hume (1711-16). The philosophical view of rational man in harmony with the universe set the climate for the "laissez-faire" economics of Adam Smith (1723-90) and for the utilitarianism of Jeremy Bentham (1748-1832) of the greatest good for the greatest number. Historical writing gained secular detachment in the work of Edward Gibbon (1737-94). In Germany, the universities became centers of the Enlightenment *(Aufklarung)*. Moses Mendelssohn (1729-86) set forth a doctrine of rational process; Gotthold Ephraim Lessing (1729-81), whom Johann Wolfgang von Goethe (1749-1832) credited as having placed the young poet in the true path, advanced a natural religion of morality; J G Herder (1744-1803) developed a philosophy of cultural nationalism. The supreme importance of the individual formed the basis of the ethics of Immanuel Kant (1724-1804). The movement received strong support of the rising bourgeoisie and vigorous opposition from the high clergy and the nobility.

The strongest claim by the West on modernity is derived from ideas and concepts generally grouped under the category of the Enlightenment. These are ideas that were developed during the half a century preceding the French Revolution, between 1740 and 1789, known in history as the Age of Enlightenment. It was at the time that the idea of progress gained popular acceptance in the West. It was a time when Europeans emerged from a long twilight, from which the past was considered barbaric and dark. This was the age of enlightened thinkers, known as *philosophes,* and enlightened despots.

The idea of the Enlightenment was drawn from earlier sources, carried over from the old philosophy of natural law, which held that right depends on a universal reason, not on local conditions or on the will or perspective of any person or group. It carried over, from the intellectual revolution of the previous century, the ideas of Bacon and Locke, Descartes and Newton, Bayle and Spinoza. It was antagonistic and skeptical toward tradition, confident in the powers of science and places faith firmly in the regularity of nature. It most serious shortcoming was the assumption that European values derived from European experience were universal truth and that such truth gave license to world dominance: the rest of the world, to escape domination and exploitation, must adopt Western ways of militarism and exploitation. The modernization of Japan was a perfect example of this trend.

The *philosophes* of the Enlightenment were mostly popularizers, in an age when the great books were not read by the public. They reworded the ideas of past civilizations in ways that held the interest of the growing reading public. These *philosophes* were primarily men of letters, exemplified by Francois Marie Arouet de Voltaire (1694-1778), who made fortunes and gained fame with his writings. They differed from intellectuals of the past who were mostly proteges of aristocratic or royal patrons or clerics in the Church.

The emergence of a literate middle class made such freelancers possible. Naturally, as most writers who enjoy popularity write what their audiences like to hear, what economist John Galbraith calls "conventional wisdom", the Enlightenment authors mostly wrote to enhance the political and economic interests of the bourgeoisie. Most of the works produced during this period focused on the catalogue and organization of information, made entertaining with wit and lightness. This was the age of the *salon literati,* of clever one-upmanship and satire, full of innuendos and sly digs, particularly insider jokes understood only by the enlightened few. Voltaire attacked European society by making fun not of the French, but by stereotyping the Persians, the Iroquois and the Chinese.

Frederick the Great of Prussia was regarded as an eminent *philosophe* through his friendship with Voltaire, whose style he emulated, as was Catherine the Great of Russia (1762-96). While Maria Teresa of Austria (1740-80) was not a *philosophe* on account of her piety, her son Joseph, brother of the ill-fated Marie-Antoinette of France (1755-93), worked hard to become one, as a patron of Wolfgang Amadeus Mozart. In England, Bishop Warburton (1698-1779) tried to become one by claiming that the Church of England as a social institution was exactly what pure reason would have invented. Edward Gibbon (1737-94), whose *Decline and Fall of the Roman Empire* summarized the millennium following the birth of Christ as "the triumph of barbarism and religion", much as the centuries after the Renaissance are summarized today as the triumph of capitalistic democracy over socialist revolutions as a religious truth. Gibbon was counted as a *philosophe* for his secular

159

outlook.

Dr Samuel Johnson (1709-84) was not considered a *philosophe*. He was fascinated by the supernatural, adhered to the established church, deflated pretentious authors, even declared Voltaire and Jean Jacques Rousseau (1712-78) "bad men" who should be sent to the plantations in America.

The Enlightenment was in essence French, a product of sophisticated Parisian *salons* run by the likes of Madame de Pompadour, mistress of Louis XV, lubricated by the liberal flow of French champagne. Denis Diderot (1713-84) was not only a card-carrying *philosophe,* his *Encyclopedie* was described as a "reasoned dictionary" written by a distinguished list of other *philosophes* who went on to enjoy the awesome rank of Encyclopedists. Another group of *philosophes* was the Physiocrats, whom critics derisively called "economists" who concerned themselves with fiscal and monetary reform, with measures to increase the national wealth of France. Among the Physiocrats were Francois Quesnay (1694-1774), physician to Louis XV (1715-74), and Dupont de Nemour (1739-1817), whose descendants became the US industrial/chemical Dupont family.

The three giants of the *philosophes* were Montesquieu, Voltaire and Rousseau. Charles Louis de Secondat, baron de la Brede et de Montesquieu (1533-92), a landed aristocrat, was a defender of his class interest. Among his associates was the Count of Boulainvilliers (1658-1722), who held that French nobility was descended from a

160

superior Germanic race, a view that contributed to the emergence of racism in the West.

In his *The Spirit of Laws* (1748), Montesquieu developed two principal ideas. One was that forms of government varied according to climate and circumstances, for example that despotism was suited more to large empires in hot climates and that democracy only would work in small city-states. Thus democracy is inconsistent with the idea of empire. The other idea was the separation and balance of powers. In France, he believed that power should be divided between the king and a number of "intermediate bodies" - parliaments, provincial estates, organized nobility, chartered towns, and even the church. It was natural for Montesquieu, a judge in parliament, a provincial and a landed nobleman, and reasonable for him to recognize the position of the bourgeoisie of the towns, but as for the Church he observed that while he took no stock in its teachings, he thought is useful as an offset to undue centralization of government. Montesquieu admired the unwritten English constitution as he understood it, not for its democratic qualities but in believing that England carried over, more successfully than any other European country, the feudal liberties of the Middle Ages. To Montesquieu, government should be a mixture of monarchy, aristocracy and democracy, a term representing the interests of the bourgeoisie, not the general population and definitely not workers and peasants.

The ideas of Montesquieu were well known to the drafters of the US constitution, who, because the United States at that time had no history of social institutions besides slavery, distorted the meaning of democracy and the separation of powers as defined by Montesquieu to create a political structure peculiarly suited only to US conditions. **Oh come now, does Liu really believe this or is it just a unique personal form of pomposity?** Those who now claim that the US version of democracy is a heritage of the Enlightenment universally suited for all humankind have been highly selective in their understanding of history.

Strictly speaking, the modern world arrived in the 18th and 19th centuries with the transfer of power from the aristocracy and the absolutist kings (Louis XIV in France and James I in England) to the upper middle classes - the elite bourgeoisie. The upper middle classes were represented by constitutional assemblies, legislatures, and parliaments, which took power away from the kings and aristocrats by violent revolutions or by reform legislation: England (1688, 1830s), the United States (1776), France (1789, 1830, 1848, 1870), Canada (1840s and 1850s), and Germany (1848, 1918). Japan embarked on a deliberate program of "modernization" in the late 19th century and early 20th century.

The shift of power was accompanied by the Industrial Revolution and liberal, or free-enterprise, economic theory (laissez faire), the economic counterpart of the middle-class political revolutions. Critiques of this modern, elitist middle-class, democratic, and laissez-faire industrial system emerged at various points in the 19th century, most notably in Marxist and other socialist movements. Although these movements of the working people were critical of the upper-middle-class entrepreneurs who led the 18th century and early 19th century "modern" revolutions, Marxists and other socialists remained modern in most of their assumptions. Thorough-going critique of the modern world view and its rational-scientific outlook, its rationally organized economic production system, and its rationally centralized bureaucratic politics did not emerge until the late 19th century and early 20th century. Such critique came at first only from philosophers such as Friedrich Nietzsche (1844-1900), scientists such as Albert Einstein (1879-1955), Sigmund Freud (1856-1939), and artists and writers. Only in the late 20th century did such postmodern critique become widespread. For most people in the 1980s, in Europe and North America and increasingly around the world, modern ways of life dominated, although intellectuals had been attacking or reinterpreting modern views for some time.

One way to understand Western modernity is to look at countervailing social, political and religious manifestations. As anthropologists, sociologists and historians have studied the "traditional village societies" that survived in a few remote areas of Europe and in non-Western cultures, they have learned much about the nature of the modern Western world view. The very name "traditional society" focuses on what is perhaps the most important single aspect. "Modern" means "now" - a world view focusing on the now, on the latest, on the newest and the most dominant. A traditional society takes "handed down" things (Latin *tradita*) as its starting point and modifies them slowly even as it tries to be faithful to the inherited ideas and customs. A modern world view implicitly assumes the superiority of the latest and newest

163

as liberating and expansive, and almost invariably scorns the old-fashioned as constrictive and oppressive. The confrontation of the non-Western world with the ascending West that turned out to be aggressively intrusive, and the rationalization of victimization as a deserved fate of not being modern, has affected the development of the non-Western world, particularly the ancient cultures found in China, India and the Middle East. It forced these cultures to reject age-old values that had evolved from centuries of struggle toward harmony to adopt the new barbarism of domination, militarism and racism to survive.

The clearest example is Japan, the thoroughly "modern" Asian power. The Meiji era (1868-1912), a period historians identify as the beginning of modern Japan, marks the reign of the Meiji emperor during which Japan was "modernized" and rose to world power status on a path that eventually brought it the detonation of two atomic bombs. The Meiji Restoration ended the more than 250-year-old feudalistic Tokugawa shogunate. In 1868, 14-year-old Mutsuhito succeeded his father, the Emperor Komei, taking the title Meiji, meaning ironically "enlightened rule". Considering that the economic structure and production of the country was then roughly equivalent to Elizabethan England, to have become a world power in such a short amount of time is widely regarded as remarkable progress. This process was closely guided and heavily subsidized by the Meiji government, enhancing the power of the great *zaibatsu,* firms such as Mitsubishi. Hand in hand, the *zaibatsu* and government developed the modern nation, borrowing technology and cultural concepts from the West, copying the British Empire of the Victorian age, much the same way Japan did from Tang China in nation-building in the 7th century. Kyoto was a scaled-down replica of the Tang capital, Changan. Japanese mercantilist policies gradually took control of much of Asia's markets for manufactures, beginning with textiles. The economic structure became mercantilist, importing raw materials and exporting finished products - a reflection of Japan's relative poverty in raw materials, a condition similar to those found in England.

Japan's defeat of China in Korea in the Sino-Japanese War (1894-95) established it not as an Asian power, but as a Western power in Asia infatuated with Western racist values, which generated much anti-Japanese sentiment throughout Asia. Japan's breakthrough as an international power came with its victory against Europeanized Russia in Manchuria in the Russo-Japanese War of 1904-05. Allied with Britain since 1902 against Czarist Russian expansionism in Asia, Japan joined the Allies in World War I, seizing German-held territory in China and the Pacific in the process, but otherwise remained largely out of the conflict. After the war, a weakened Europe left a greater share in international markets to the United States and Japan, both of which emerged greatly strengthened, setting them on a path of conflict that ended in Pearl Harbor. Japanese competition made great inroads into hitherto European-dominated markets in Asia, not only in China, but also even in European colonies such as British India and Dutch Indonesia.

Japan emerged from the Tokugawa-Meiji transition as the first industrialized nation in Asia. Domestic commercial activities and limited foreign trade had met the demands for material culture in the Tokugawa period, but the modernized Meiji era had radically different requirements. From the onset, the Meiji rulers embraced the concept of a market economy and adopted British and American forms of free-enterprise capitalism. The private sector - in a nation blessed with an abundance of aggressive entrepreneurs - welcomed such change. Trade in the Confucian culture that formed Japan ranked below prostitution in social esteem. Luckily for the merchant class, trade was rescued from traditional social scorn through its role in national survival. Similar evolution is currently taking place in China, with results that are controversial at best.

Economic reforms included a unified modern currency based on the yen, banking, commercial and tax laws, stock exchanges, and a communications network. Establishment of a modern institutional framework conducive to an advanced capitalist economy took time but was put in place by the 1890s. By this time, the government had largely relinquished direct control of the modernization process, primarily for budgetary reasons. Many of the former *daimyo,* whose pensions had been paid in a lump sum, benefited greatly through investments they made in emerging industries. Those who had been informally involved in foreign trade before the Meiji Restoration also flourished. Old *bakufu*-serving firms that clung to their traditional ways failed in the new business environment.

The establishment of the *bakufu* by Minamoto Yoritomo was the single most transforming event of early Japan. The *bakufu,* or "tent government" (because soldiers lived in tents), was more or less a military government. It primarily functioned as a separate government concerned principally with military and police matters. The emperor's government in Kyoto continued to function as before: the court still appointed civil governors, collected taxes, and exercised complete control in the area surrounding the capital.

The real power of the state, however, became more concentrated in the hands of the Kamakura shogun. The word *shogun* is a Chinese term for "general". Minamoto Yoritomo demanded the title *Sei i tai shogun,* "barbarian-conquering great general", when he defeated the Taira. The shogun, and the military government beneath him, really did not control much of Japan. For all practical purposes, the provinces of Japan were independent even though local lords *(daimyo)* who swore allegiance to the shogun.

The shogunate, however, did not remain in Minamoto clan hands for very long. When Yoritomo died in 1199, his widow, from the clan of the Hojo, usurped power from the Minamoto clan. She was a Buddhist nun, so she became known as the "Nun Shogun". She displaced the son who had inherited from his father and installed another son, who was soon assassinated. From that point onward, the Hojo clan ruled the *bakufu* while the Minamoto clan nominally occupied the position of shogun. The relationship between the *bakufu* and the imperial government had never been very friendly; in 1221, the imperial court led an uprising against the *bakufu,* but failed. By this point, however, the ideology of loyalty had become fully ingrained in the bakufu structure; the imperial court had little success persuading people to break that loyalty.

The defining moment for the Kamakura *bakufu* was the unsuccessful invasion of Japan by the Mongol Chinese. In 1258, Kublai Khan conquered the Korean Peninsula and in 1266, he declared himself emperor of China and established the Yuan Dynasty. In 1266, representatives of the Yuan court came to Japan and demanded submission to Chinese rule. The imperial court was terrified, but the Hojo clan decided to stand its ground and sent the representatives home. In 1274, the Yuan emperor sent a vast fleet to invade Japan but it was destroyed by a hurricane - the Japanese called this fortunate hurricane *kamikaze,* or "wind from the gods". Again in 1281, China launched the largest amphibious assault in the history of the ancient and medieval worlds. The Chinese army was a terrifying invasion force. But the Hojo clan managed to keep the Chinese from landing by building a vast seawall against the invaders. Another hurricane again sank the Chinese fleet.

The *bakufu* might have saved Japan from Chinese invasion, but they could not survive the modernization program of the Meiji Restoration. The Meiji government was initially involved in economic modernization, providing a number of "model factories" to facilitate the transition to the modern period. After the first two decades of the Meiji period, the industrial economy expanded rapidly until about 1920 with inputs of advanced Western technology and large private investments. Stimulated by wars and through cautious economic planning, Japan emerged from World War I as a major industrial nation. Its mercantilist path led it to the quest of empire in the British fashion. After World War II, General Douglas MacArthur turned Japan into an export dynamo in the service of the United States in the context of the Cold War. This role became obsolete after the end of the Cold War. The current economic crisis in Japan is rooted in issues much deeper than Western economists have identified.

Europeans outside of Italy were much less conscious of any sudden break with the Middle Ages. Medieval intellectual interests persisted in the continuing founding of universities, which the Italian humanists regarded as pedantic centers of scholastic learning. Between 1386 and 1506, no fewer than 14 universities were founded in Germany, while no new university was founded in Italy in the 15th century. At one of the new German universities, at Wittenburg, founded in 1502, Marin Luther (1484-1546) launched the Reformation against the Renaissance Church. The Scholastic philosophy of Thomas Aquinas (1225-74) laid the foundation of European thought by calling for exactness and disciplined thinking, and above all made Christendom safe for reason with his doctrine that faith could not be endangered by reason. In contrast, at about the same time, Islamic authorities ruled that valid interpretation of the Koran had ended with the Four Great Doctors of early Islam. "The gate was closed" was an Islamic saying, and with it centuries of brilliant Arabic thought withered away gradually. It is the greatest irony in intellectual history, since it had been Arabic learning on ancient Greek culture that helped Christian scholars rediscover Aristotelian syllogism.

The Holy Roman Empire was proclaimed in AD 962, five decades after the German magnates elected a king in 911, who also assumed the title of Holy Roman Emperor. The Holy Roman Empire was in theory coterminous with Latin Christendom, and endowed with a special mission of defending and extending the true faith. The Holy Roman Emperor was never able to consolidate his political domain as did the kings of France and England, because the magnates of Germany allied themselves with the papacy in Rome to preserve their feudal liberties from the emperor.

In the mid-15th century, a group of kings in Europe, known in history as the New Monarchs, succeeded in laying the foundation for nation-states. The new

170

monarchs offered the institution of monarchy as a guarantee of law and order, against aristocratic abuse of the bourgeoisie and the peasants who were willing to pay taxes to the king in return for peace and protection, and to let the king dominate parliament, which had proved to be a stronghold of the aristocracy. The new monarchies broke down the mass of inherited feudal "common law" through which the rights of the feudal classes were entrenched, by reinstituting Roman law, which was actively studied in the new universities. These new monarchs proclaimed themselves as sovereigns and required their subjects to address them as "Your Majesty." According to *lex regia* in Roman law, the sovereign incorporates the will and the welfare of the people in his person, and upholds the principle of *salus populi suprema lex* (the welfare of the people is the highest law). The sovereign can make law, enact it by his own authority regardless of past customs or historical liberties by the principle of *quo principi placuit legis habet vigorem* (what pleases the prince has the force of law).

The New Monarchy came to England with the dynasty of the Tudors, whose first king, Henry VII (1485-1509), put an end to the War of the Roses, which had greatly decimated the English baronial families. In France, the New Monarchy was represented by Louis XI (1461-83) and his successors. Louis XI maintained a regular royal army, no longer dependent on aristocratic support for maintaining peace and waging war. The French king acquired much greater authority to raise taxes without parliament consent than the English Tudors. The Estate General met only once in the reign of Louis XI, and on that occasion requested the king to govern without them in the future. Over the First Estate, the Church, the French kings asserted extensive powers.

The Pragmatic Sanction of 1438 gave the Gallic Church much independence from Rome. In 1516, King Francis I reached an agreement with Pope Leo X, the Concordat of Bologna, rescinding the Pragmatic Sanction, by dividing the independence with Rome receiving the "innates" or money income from French ecclesiastics, the king appointed the bishops and abbots. The fact that the French monarchy controlled the Gallic church was the main reason why France never turned Protestant.

The New Monarchy came to Spain through facilities offered by the Church, since the kingdom of Spain did not exist before that. The Spanish were the most tolerant of all Europeans, with Christians, Muslims and Jews living in harmony. As the New Monarchy in Spain followed a religious bent, achieving unification through the Church, national feelings fused with Catholicity. With the Christian conquest of Granada, Moors and Jews were expelled. The Inquisition hunted down Moriscos (Christians with Moorish background) and Maranos (Christians of Jewish background). A decree in 1492 expelling Jews followed their expulsion from England in 1290 and from France in 1306. Jews were not allowed to return to England until the mid-17th century and to France until after the French Revolution. The Sephardic Jews from Spain went mostly to the Near and Middle East. The Jews who left England and France went mostly to Germany, the great center of Ashkenazic Jewry of the Middle Ages. Driven from Germany in the 14th century, they concentrated in Poland until the Holocaust of the 1940s.

Ideas of the New Monarchy were also at work in the Holy Roman Empire in Germany, with the difference that the estates in the other new monarchies took the form of princely states, duchies, margraviats, bishoprics and abbacies in Germany. The emperor became an elective office by seven Electors. In 1356, the Archduke of Austria, a Hapsburg, was elected emperor. The Hapsburgs remained the principal power in Europe, until after the Thirty Years' War, which ended in 1648.

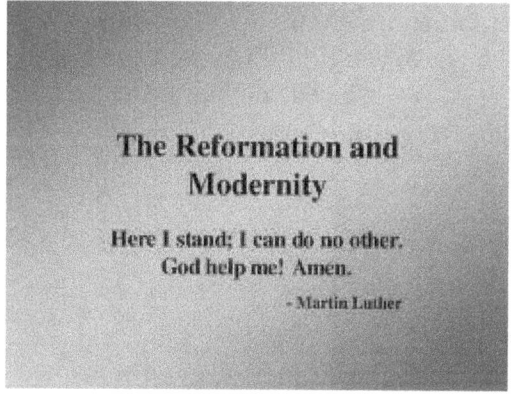

The Reformation and Modernity

Here I stand; I can do no other.
God help me! Amen.

- Martin Luther

Protestantism, as espoused by Martin Luther (1483-1546), was revolutionary because its doctrines held not merely that abuses in the Church must be reformed but that the Roman Church itself, even if perfect by its own ideals, was wrong in principle. Protestants aimed not to restore the medieval Church from Renaissance abuses, but to overthrow it and replace it with a church founded on principles drawn from the Bible. Such principles

173

should not be decreed by the Church but by the individual believer's conscience.

This attitude against central authority was music to the German princes, who responded positively to Luther's invitation to the state to assume control of religion. Protestantism became entwined with social and political revolution. Charles V, as Holy Roman Emperor, was obliged to defend the faith because only within a Catholic world did the Holy Roman Empire have any meaning. The princely states within the empire saw the emperor's effort to suppress Luther as a threat to their own freedom. The imperial free states and the dynastic states of northern Germany insisted on *ius reformandi,* the right to determine their own religion. They became Lutheran and secularized (i.e., confiscated) church properties to enrich the secular sovereigns.

Thus Luther, in placing theological protest under the protection of secular power politics, exploited the political aspirations of budding German principalities in the 16th century. In return, he conveniently provided the German princes with a theological basis for political secession from the theocratic Holy Roman Empire.

Luther exploited the political aspirations of German princes to be independent of the Holy Roman Emperor to bolster his theological revolt from the Roman Catholic Church. But he came to denounce peasant rebellions when the peasants rebelled against the Protestant German princes. He did so even though such peasant uprisings against the German princes claimed inspiration from the same theological ideas of the Reformation that had motivated the revolt against the Holy Roman Emperor by the same German princes for independence. Such radical ideas had been advocated by Luther. However, even Luther's professed personal sympathy for peasant demands for improved treatment from their oppressive princes did not persuade him to endorse peasant uprisings.

In fact, Luther could be considered a Stalinist. Or more accurately, Joseph Vissarionovich Stalin (1879-1953) would in fact fit the definition of a Lutheran diehard, at least in revolutionary strategy if not in ideological essence. Like Luther, Stalin suppressed populist radicalism to preserve institutional revolution, and glorified the state as the sole legitimate expeditor of revolutionary ideology.

Early Protestantism, like Stalinism, became more oppressive and intolerant than the system it replaced. Ironically, puritanical Protestant ethics celebrating the virtues of thrift, industry, sobriety and responsibility, were identified by many sociologists as the driving force centuries later behind the success of modern capitalism and industrialized economy. Particularly, ethics as espoused by Calvinism, which in its extreme advocated subordination of the state to the church, diverging from Luther's view of the state to which the church is subordinate, was ironically credited as the spirit behind the emergence of the modern Western industrial state. In that sense, the post-Cold War Islamic theocratic states are Calvinist in principle.

Chapter 7 - THE ABDUCTION OF MODERNITY Part 6a: Imperialism as Modernity

Imperialism is the extension of rule or dominance by one people over another. Ancient imperialism reached its climax under the Roman Empire, which collapsed in the West after two centuries of *Pax Romana,* and withered away finally in the East in the late Middle Ages with the collapse of the Byzantine Empire in 1453. The fall of Constantinople in 1453 to the Ottoman Sultan Mohammad II is viewed by some historians as the beginning of the modern age. Thereafter, imperialism subsided. Subsequently, the Holy Roman Empire and Ottoman Dominion emerged as confederations of princely states of high degrees of autonomy rather than imposed imperial rule.

A new imperialism was reborn in the West with the rise of commercial capitalism in the 17th century in which external trade became indispensable to the growth of domestic economies. Under commercial capitalism, capital was primarily employed to finance inventory and logistics, not manufacturing. Commercial capitalism was a socio-economic system characterized by private ownership of the means of distribution, not necessarily of production, operating for private profit through the institutions of private bank credit and linked distant markets.

The rise of industrial capitalism dated from the Industrial Revolution of the 18th century with the private ownership of the means of production and imposed distant markets. Nineteen-century imperialism was an extension of industrial capitalism. Neo-imperialism of the post-Cold War era is an extension of finance capitalism, in which the global manipulation of finance dominates all else. Though the specific characters of capitalism have changed over the ages, the fundamental essence of capitalism is not a product of modernity. Neither is imperialism, the political extension of capitalism.

Protestantism, particularly Calvinism, provided the spiritual foundation for the spread of industrial capitalism. Calvinism, being critical of human nature, believes that God's grace is bestowed on only a few elected godly individuals as predestination. A believer can instill in his/her own consciousness an awareness of being among the pre-selected saved, as God's chosen few, if throughout all trials and temptations, he/she persists in a saintly life. Predestination thus becomes a challenge to exert unrelenting human effort with burning religious conviction and to undertake a mission to do the battle of God, rejecting pessimism and resignation.

Predestination has its parallel in Chinese Buddhism. Looking for a politically correct Buddhist theologian, Li Shimin, a Taoist and the Genesis Emperor (Taizong) of the Tang Dynasty, found him in the person of Xuanzang (605-661), an eminent pilgrim *seng* (Buddhist monk). With imperial sponsorship, Xuanzang would in his life be the prodigious translator of *Yogacara-bhumi,* a treatise of the Yogacara school of Indian Mahayana Buddhism (Dasheng, meaning "major vehicle"), and establish a new denomination that would call itself the Faxiang sect (Methodist Divination).

Compared with the merciful theology of universal salvation in Chinese Mahayana Buddhism set by the widely recognized Tiantai sect (Heaven Platform), the Faxiang sect founded by Xuanzang is an anomaly in the development of Buddhist thought in China. After its initial flowering, it faded quickly after the withdrawal of imperial sponsorship, when subsequent sovereigns supported their own separate religious sects.

179

Xuanzang, brought up as an ecclesiastic apprentice since birth, was ordained as a *seng* at an early age in Chengdu in the western province of Sichuan. Chengdu is 1,200 kilometers east of Lhasa in Xizang (Tibet), which in turn is separated by the impassable Himalayas from Xiyu (Western District, a term Tang geographers used to include the northern regions of India, referred to as Tianshu). Like all devout and zealous *sengs* of his day, Xuanzang in his youth longed for an opportunity to go to Xiyu, birthplace of Buddhism, to seek true scripture as well as for personal enlightenment. Northern India was considered the holy land of Buddhism, known by Buddhists in Tang China as Bei Tianshu. Bei Tianshu was part of Xiyu, a general term for all regions south and west of Dunhuang, a famous site of Buddhist grotto temples in the northwestern province of Kansu, on the far western border of the Tang Empire where the southern branch of the Silk Route toward India began.

India was known as Shendu in China during the Han Dynasty (206 BC-AD 220), possibly a Chinese translation of the Sanskrit word *Hindu*. It was also known as Land of Poluomen, derived from the Sanskrit word *Brahman*. Modern Chinese refers to India as Yindu, a modification of *Hindu*. During the Tang time (618-907) it was referred to as Tianshu, a land with five separate independent kingdoms.

Young Xuanzang applied for official permission to make a pilgrimage, as required by law. But permission was denied as part of a general Taoist Tang imperial policy that discouraged further Buddhist pilgrimage. Undaunted,

180

Xuanzang went surreptitiously on his own accord. In his extensive pilgrimage, Xuanzang was aided by many pious local Buddhist lords and officials who passively opposed Taoist imperial anti-Buddhist policies, paying only lip service to the thin authority of the Tang court in religious matters.

In the Tang time, the journey from China to Xiyu was circuitous and difficult, having to cross the Tarim Basin desert, passing Samarkand in Turkistan and Kabul in Afghanistan, and through Kashmir to reach northern India. Direct access through Xizang (Tibet) was physically hazardous because of the forbidding height of the Himalaya mountain ranges that separate China and India. It was also politically treacherous because of the relentless hostility of the Tufans (Tibetans), one of several branches of the Western Rong Barbarians known as Xiqiang.

Nevertheless, Xuanzang managed to arrive in northern India with a small entourage of faithful servants who were social outcasts back home. He traveled to the southern tip of the Indian subcontinent via the east coast and returned north via the west coast. In India, Xuanzang spent almost 15 years studying, five of which at Nalanda, an important center of Buddhism in northeastern India, with the brilliant but highly unorthodox elder, Silabhadra. A relatively minor figure in the Yogacara school of Indian Mahayana Buddhism (Dasheng), Silabhadra was not particularly known for having represented faithfully the teachings of Vasubandhu, the recognized authoritative Yogacara philosopher.

The most crucial aspect of Silabhadra's heretical offshoot theology is the assertion that only some select persons would reach eventual enlightenment, and, in fact, there is a whole category of people for whom attainment to Buddhahood is impossible. Furthermore, through no fault of their own, these unfortunate souls inherently lack untainted seeds, and hence are eternally excluded from salvation. The best that such pathetic souls in this unfortunate category of deficient people could hope for would be continuing cycles of ameliorative rebirth, which fortunately could still be achieved through the accumulation of spiritual merits.

This unorthodox and unmerciful idea of predestination was brought back to China by Xuanzang in the 7th century. Unlike Calvinism in the West, Xuanzang's Faxiang sect did not flourish in China. Taoists challenge Buddhist precepts with obvious demographic evidence on the discrepancy between the spread of Buddhism and the persistent increase of misery in the world's growing population. Buddhism, of course, has never proposed any program for elimination of secular misery. It merely promises to make such misery less painful spiritually. To the enlightened Buddhist, both extreme wealth and extreme poverty are curses.

Gunnar Myrdal (1898-1984), a Swedish sociologist-economist born 12 centuries after Xuanzang, in his 1944 definitive study *The American Dilemma,* for which he received the 1974 Nobel Prize for Economics, having declared the "Negro" problem in the United States to be inextricably entwined with the democratic functioning of American society, went on to produce a 1976 study of Southeast Asia, *The Asian Dilemma.* In it, he identified Buddhist acceptance of suffering as the prime cause for economic underdevelopment in the region. Myrdal's conclusion appears valid superficially, given the coincident of indisputable existence of conditions of poverty in the region at the time of his study and the pervasive influence of Buddhism in Southeast Asian culture, until the question is asked as to why, whereas Buddhism has prevailed in Southeast Asia for more than a millennium, pervasive poverty in the region would only make its appearance after the arrival of Western

183

imperialism in the 19th century. It could be that Myrdal had been influenced in his convenient conclusion by his eagerness to deflect responsibility for the sorry state of affairs in the region from the legacy of Western imperialism.

In contrast to Lutherans, who glorify the state as the sole legitimate expeditor of revolutionary ideology, Calvinists reject the subordination of church to state and embrace the holy mission to Christianize the state. Calvinism rejects democracy with its elitist outlook. While the ideas of Calvinism were central to the rise of capitalism, these ideas fostered in early capitalism a mission to create a religious community that celebrated ascetic living for all, devoid of greed and the exploitative elements that permeate modern capitalism. Calvinists were called Puritans first in England and later in America.

The economic dimensions of Protestantism - acquisitiveness, aggressiveness, competitiveness and capitalistic exploitation - legitimized by religious righteousness, dismantled the self-restraint on individualism and greed that early Christianity tried to foster and medieval Christianity tried to institutionalize. Protestantism plunged the world into centuries of disharmony, war and conflict in the name of modernity. **Wow, I believe Calvin would rollover in his grave if he were to hear that his reformation of the Catholic Church sparked centuries of warfare and disharmony. Common Sense should tell you rather than history that this is pure fantasy. It is also obvious to me that Liu has very little knowledge of**

184

Calvin's belief in predestination nor does he understand the virtues of Protestantism.

The Arabs, a people generally defined by a common Arabic language, awakened with the new faith of Islam by Mohammed (died 632), took control of Syria, Mesopotamia, Persia and Egypt in 640, took Roman Africa in 700 and reached Spain in 711, where they overthrew the Germanic kingdom set up by the West Goths. The Arab realm then stood as the advanced third component of a triangulated non-Asian world culture of Byzantines, Arabs and the collapsed Roman West. The latter had been overran by uncouth Germanic tribes who had yet to develop written languages and who settled disputes with trials by battle, known as ordeals. Europe was in what historians call the Dark Ages. In the aftermath of the fall of the Western Roman Empire, with *Pax Romana* in ruins, while the Eastern Roman emperors, ruling from Constantinople, kept a dim light of Roman civilization burning, in the West that light flickered and went out except in the network of fortified monasteries that rejected the barbaric society at large.

From 800 to 1500, during the European Dark Ages, significant advances in philosophy, literature and poetry and discoveries in mathematics, medicine, astronomy and science were made by scholars in the Arab world. During this period of seven centuries, almost all scientific texts were written in Arabic, and the discoveries of Arab thinkers of this period laid the very foundations from which both Scholasticism and the Renaissance would emerge. Advances in mathematics as well as scientific methods of detailed and systematic observation of nature

185

in this period by Arabs contributed to the later intellectual growth that propelled the Western world through the Industrial and Scientific revolutions. In learning, the Arabs preserved Greek civilization neglected by the Western barbarians. William Shakespeare, in *Julius Caesar*, has Casca reporting to Brutus on Cicero, who spoke in Greek: "Those that understood him smiled at one another and shook their heads; but for mine own part, it was Greek to me." The year before (1600), another Elizabethan playwright, Thomas Dekker, wrote: "I'll be sworn he knows not so much as one character of the tongue. Why, then it's Greek to him." The phrase came from a medieval Latin proverb, *"Graecum est; non potest legi"* (It is Greek; it cannot be read). The Spanish version of this proverb is *"hablar en griego"*, which is commonly said to be the origin of the word *gringo*, one who is literally accused of speaking Greek, and hence being unintelligible.

The Arabs went beyond what the ancient Greeks had achieved. They invented Arabic numerals, the concept of zero (Arabic *sifr*), and algebra (*al-jebr-jabara*), on which modern mathematics and science flowered. Roman numerals, in their cumbersome form, would have never led to the development of advanced mathematics. Some other English words of Arabic origin are "admiral" *(amir-al-bahr)*, "adobe" *(al-toba)*, "alchemy" *(al-kimia)*, "alcohol" *(al-kohl)*, "algorithm" *(al-Khowarazmi)*, "alkali" *(al-qaliy)*, "almanac" (Andalucian Arabic *al-manakh*), "amber" *('anbar)*, "antimony" *(al-ithmid)*, "apricot" *(al-burquq)*, "arsenal" *(dar assina'ah)*, "artichoke" *(al-kharshuf)*, "assassin" *(h'ashshashin)*, "azure" *(al-lazward)*, "caliber" *(qalib)*, "checkmate" *(shah mat)*, cipher *(sifr)*, "cork" *(qurq)*, "cotton" *(qutn)*, "crimson" *(qirmazi)*, "elixir" *(al-iksir)*, "jar" *(jarrah)*, "jasmine" *(yasmin)*, "lilac" *(lilak)*, "lemon" *(laymun)*, "lime" *(limah)*, "lute" *(al-'ud)*, "magazine" *(makhazin)*, "mask" *(maskhara)*, "mattress" *(matrah)*, "mohair" *(mukhayyar)*, "monsoon" *(mausim)*, "nadir" *(nadir)*, "orange" *(naranj)*, "safari" *(safariy)*, "saffron" *(za'faran)*, "sofa" *(suffah)*, "sugar" *(sukkar)*, "syrup" *(sharab)*, "tariff" *(tarif)*, "tarragon" *(tarkhun)*, and "zenith" *(samt)*. Yet for all its cultural achievements, the Arabs, not unlike the Germans until the 19th century, were prevented by their tribal culture from developing a unified central political entity.

By the mid-16th century, the Holy Roman Empire under the Hapsburgs took on the characteristics of a universal monarchy in parallel to the Roman Church's claim of catholic religion. France, a Catholic nation in good standing, to contain the Hapsburgs' expanding control of Spain, the Netherlands, Germany, Austria, Italy and Greece, allied itself with the rebelling Protestant German states and even the "infidel" Ottoman Empire against the Hapsburg Holy Roman emperors.

The Ottomans developed one of the greatest and most influential civilizations in history. Their moment of glory in the 16th century represented one of the heights of human creativity, optimism and artistic achievement, weaving the diverse strands of several cultures, from Greek to Romanesque to Arabic to Anatolian, into an Ottoman civilization under the spiritual unity of Islam. Their system of rule, a form of dominion of diverse ethnicities, religions and cultures, misnamed "empire" by

187

the West, was the largest and most influential of the Muslim world, and their culture and military expansion crossed over into Europe. There was no wholesale compulsory conversion of Christians or Jews into Muslims. Christians under Ottoman rule fared better than Muslims did under Christendom, or Moors in Spain, or Protestants in France or Catholics in England and Ireland. The Ottoman Dominion, which by 1650 extended from the Hungarian plains and the southern Russian steppes as far as Algeria, the upper Nile and the Persian Gulf, lasted until the 20th century, ending with the secularization of a Westernized Turkey after World War I along a European model of government.

By 1400, the Ottomans had extended their control over much of Anatolia and into Byzantine territory in Eastern Europe: Macedonia and Bulgaria. In 1402, the Ottomans moved their capital to Edirne in southeastern Europe, where they threatened the last great bastion of the Byzantine Empire, its capital, Constantinople. In 1453, Sultan Mehmed (1451-81), who was called "The Conqueror". took this one last remnant of Byzantium and renamed it Istanbul. From that point onward, the capital of the Ottoman Dominion would remain in Istanbul and, under the patronage of the Ottoman sultans, would become one of the richest and most cultured cities in history.

Ottoman rule expanded greatly under Sultan Selim I (1512-20). Under Sultan Suleyman (1520-66), called "The Lawmaker" in Islamic history and "The Magnificent" in Europe, the rule reached its greatest expansion over Asia and Europe. The Ottomans inherited a rich mixture of cultural traditions and political structure from disparate civilizations and ethnic groups - Turks, Arabs, Persians, Mongols and Mesopotamian - unified by Islam. The Ottoman state, like other states in the region and, in similar ways, like the Chinese state and the European New Monarchs, rested on a principle of absolute authority of the monarch. The nature of Ottoman autocracy, however, has been fundamentally misunderstood and misinterpreted with prejudice in the West.

The central function of the ruler, or sultan, in Ottoman political theory was to guarantee justice ('*adale* in Arabic) in the Dominion. All authority hinges on the ruler's personal commitment to justice. This idea has Turco-Persian, Arabic and Islamic aspects. In Islamic political theory, the model of a just ruler was Solomon in Hebrew history (Suleyman was named after Solomon). The justice represented by the Solomonic ruler is a distributive justice; this is a justice of fairness and equity. In addition, '*adale* has Turco-Persian-Arabic coordinates. In this tradition, '*adale* starts with the protection of the helpless from the rapacity of corrupt and predatory forces in society and government.

In this sense, justice involves protecting the lowest members of society, the peasantry, from predatory exploitation, unfair taxation, corrupt magistracy, and inequitable courts. This, in Ottoman political theory, was the primary task of the sultan, who personally protected his people from the excesses of society and government, corruption of local officials and abuse from the privileged classes. It is the equivalent of the Chinese Confucian

189

concept of a Mandate of Heaven to rule, which is based on an obligation to protect the welfare of the people. The ruler could only guarantee this justice if he had absolute power, lest he should be restricted by a structural balance of power and so subject to corruption by special-interest groups. The cooptation of government by special-interest groups is the gravest weakness of Western representative democracy. Alexis de Tocqueville (1805-59) predicted accurately that equality in early US society would eventually be endangered by the domination of its political system by a new industrial/financial class.

Absolute authority was justified in building a just and virtuous government and an equitable system of law rather than elevating the ruler above the law, as Europeans generally misinterpreted the sultanate by mislabeling it as despotism. This predestination of the sultanate has commonality in principle with the predestination of Calvinism. It parallels the rationale of European absolute monarchy, the authority of the king resting on his divine duty to protect the peasants from aristocratic abuse. The concept of virtue as a foundation of temporal power was operative in medieval Europe. During the French Revolution, the controversial Maximilian Robespierre believed in the dictatorship of "virtue" in a political order. Both Montesquieu and Jean-Jacques Rousseau held that good governance rests on "virtue" - the unselfish public spirit and civic zeal exemplified by personal uprightness and purity of both the governor and the governed. The Confucian theory of a Mandate of Heaven to rule is based on the concept of virtue. The Western democracies, with their abduction of the concept of modernity, are not detached from this timeless notion of good governance, as expressed in the doctrine of sovereignty.

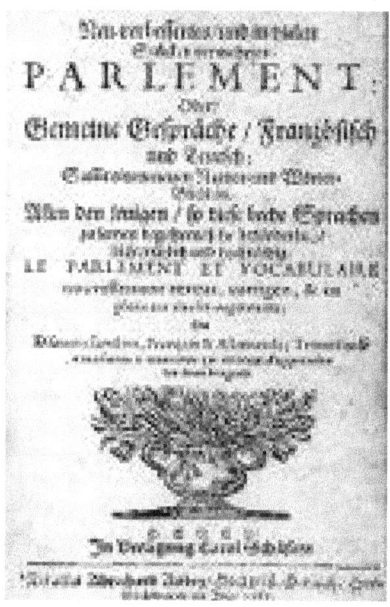

Jean Bodin (1530-96), the first to develop the theory of sovereignty in the West, held that in every society there must be one power with the legitimate authority to give law to all others. The Edict of Nantes issued by Henry IV in 1598 was a sovereign edict to protect a Huguenot (French Calvinist) minority, composed mostly of members of the aristocracy, against popular opposition from the Catholic peasants. The Edict led to the assassination of the king by a Catholic fanatic in 1610. The widowed queen, Marie de Medicis, handed control of France to Cardinal Richelieu, who undertook a secular policy to enhance the economic interest of the state with mercantilist measures, by allowing the aristocracy to engage in maritime trade without loss of noble status, and making it possible for merchants to become nobles by payments to the royal exchequer. This provided a political union of the aristocracy and the bourgeois elite that held the nation together until the French Revolution. In 1627, the Duke of Rohan led a Huguenot rebellion from La Rochelle with English military support. Richelieu suppressed the rebellion ruthlessly and modified the Edict of Nantes with the Peace of Alais in 1629, by allowing the Huguenots to keep their religion but stripping them of their instruments of political power: their fortified cities, their Protestant armies and all their military and territorial autonomy and rights.

The Age of New Monarchy in Europe laid the foundation for the Age of Nation States by placing royal authority above feudal rights, a development that began in the High Middle Ages. The new monarchs offered the institution of monarchy as a guarantor of law and order and promoted hereditary monarchy as the legitimate means of transferring public power. Monarchism was supported by the urban bourgeoisie, as they had long been victimized by the private wars and marauding excesses of the feudal lords. The bourgeoisie was willing to pay taxes directly to the king in return for peace and protection from aristocratic abuse. Its members were willing to let parliament, the stronghold of the aristocracy, be dominated by the king. The direct collection of popular taxes by the king, bypassing the feudal lords, gave the king the necessary resources to maintain a standing army to keep the feudal lords in check. These new monarchs revived Roman law, which favors the state and incorporates the will and welfare of the people in their own persons.

The new monarchies, by breaking down feudal tariff barriers within the kingdom, contributed to the rise of the commercial revolution and the development of extended cross-border markets. In the rise of capitalism, the needs of the military had been (and still are) of critical importance. The standing national armies of the new monarchs required sudden expenditures in times of war that the normal flow of tax revenue could not meet. Private bankers emerged to finance wars by lending the kings money secured by the future collection of taxes from conquered lands. The medieval prohibition of interest as usury, denounced as the sin of avarice and forbidden by canon law, continued to be upheld by all religions. Luther denounced "Fruggerism" in reference to the bankers of the Holy Roman Empire. Even Calvinism only gradually made allowances on the issue of interest. The new monarchies, caught between fixed income and mounting expenses, were forced to devalue their money by diluting its gold content. They began to borrow from private banks to deal with recurring monetary crises. The monetary crises led to constitutional crises that produced absolute monarchies in Europe and the triumph of bourgeois parliamentarianism in England.

The Bank of Amsterdam, established in 1609, issued gold florins of known and fixed purity, which quickly assumed the status of international reserve currency for financing trade and wars, making Amsterdam an international finance center until the fall of Napoleon Bonaparte. The arrival of vast amounts of gold into Spain from its American colonies in the 17th century greatly increased the European specie money supply that fueled the growth of Europe and caused a wave of gold inflation that had economic and constitutional consequences. European rulers became hard-pressed for money, and needed more as their currencies fell in value.

Their common desire to force gold and silver to flow into their separate kingdoms found expression in mercantilism which involved "putting the poor to work", as the English put it, to reap the full benefit of industrialization. Mercantilism became in the economic sphere what nation-building of the new monarchies was in the political. Industrial policies nurtured new industries within every kingdom. A silk industry was brought from Italy to France under royal protection. The migration of skilled Flemish weavers to England was induced and supervised by the Crown to turn England from a producer of raw wool to an exporter of finished woolens. The king even authorized the abduction of two youths who knew advanced dyeing arts from faraway Ottoman regions. France signed treaties with the Ottoman rulers in 1535 to grant French merchants special privileges, including extraterritoriality, called capitulations, in the Ottoman Dominion. A capitulation treaty with England was signed in 1579, the Netherlands in 1598, Russia in 1768, Austria in 1780 and finally with Italy and Germany in the 19th century.

The Peace of Westphalia of 1648 that ended the Thirty Years' War blocked the Counter-Reformation, contained expanding Hapsburg supremacy and forestalled German unification for two centuries. It also heralded the age of sovereign states in Europe in a *Staatensystem* held together by the doctrine of balance of power. It arrested aspiration for a universal state in Europe until the formation of the European Union four centuries later. It also formally recognized Calvinism. Out of the peace rose *Le Grand Monarque* in the person of the Sun King, Louis XIV of France. Crowned at the age of five, assuming control of government at the age of 23, and reigning for 72 years until his death in 1715, Louis XIV ruled longer than any other monarch in modern history. France rose to challenge the universal monarchy status of the Holy Roman Empire of the Hapsburgs. Europe as a whole, stabilized by the balance of power of the Peace of Westphalia, was able to focus on expansion beyond Europe.

Balance of power in geopolitics refers to the orchestration of an international equilibrium of state power. If one power predominates, as the Holy Roman Empire did in the 16th century, other states may form a coalition to counterweigh it. Or, if a state is a virtually necessary member of a coalition, more needed by its allies than it is in need of them, it may be said to hold the balance, or if a state belong to no coalition at all, but its intervention on one side or the other would be decisive in tilting the balance. The general rule of "the enemy of my enemy is my friend" governs the game of balance of power. Ideology takes a back seat in international balance-of-power geopolitics.

Suleyman became a major player in 16th-century European balance-of-power geopolitics by pursuing an aggressive policy toward European destabilization, in reaction to European expansionism. In particular, he aimed to destabilize both the Roman Catholic Church and the Holy Roman Empire and to contain their parallel expansion. When Christianity split Europe into Catholic and Protestant states, Suleyman poured financial support into Protestant countries in order to guarantee that Europe remain religiously and politically divided. Some historians argue that Protestantism would never have succeeded except for the financial support of the Ottomans (S A Fisher-Galati: *Ottoman Imperialism and German Protestantism, 1521-1555*).

Henry II of France recognized the need for France to maintain an Ottoman alliance against Charles V, the Hapsburg Holy Roman emperor. The French alliance was the cornerstone of Ottoman policy on Europe, buttressed by the natural alliance with the Schmalkalden League of the German Protestant princes fighting to gain political independence from the Holy Roman Empire with the help of theological divergence. At the instigation of the French, Suleyman urged the German princes to cooperate with France against the pope and the emperor. He also assured them of amnesty from Ottoman conquest. Ottoman pressure during the three decades between 1521 and 1555 forced the Hapsburgs to grant concessions to the Protestants and was a factor in the eventual official recognition, if not tolerance, of Protestantism within the Holy Roman Empire. In the 16th century, the Ottoman sultan claimed titular sovereignty over Venice, Poland and the Hapsburg Empire, on the fact that they were all tribute-paying states, and even over France when Francis I requested Ottoman aid and formed the Ottoman alliance.

What Suleyman did not realize was that in opposing an expanding Catholic threat, he unwittingly encouraged a new one, more dangerous and deadly, in the form of Protestantism and capitalistic imperialism.

Far from promoting innate expansionism, Suleyman was in actuality responding defensively to an aggressively expanding Europe in the 16th century. Like many other non-Europeans, Suleyman understood the consequences of European expansion and saw Christian Europe as the principal threat to Islam and the Islamic world, which was beginning to shrink under this expansion. Portugal had invaded several Muslim cities in East Africa in order to dominate trade with India. Russia, which the Ottomans regarded as European, was pushing Central Asians southward when the Russian expansion began in the 16th century.

With a defensive strategy of counter-invasion against and destabilization of expansionist Europe, Suleyman pursued a policy of helping any Muslim country threatened by European/Christian expansion. It was the forerunner of the Truman Doctrine to contain global communist expansion after World War II.

This predestination role gave Suleyman the right, in the eyes of the Ottomans, to declare himself the supreme caliph of Islam. As the only effective leader successfully protecting Islam from the expansionist infidels, the protector of Islam must be the ruler of the whole Islamic world, the counterpart of the Holy Roman emperor as the Defender of the Faith for Catholicism. So the clash of civilizations began long before the recent observations of Samuel Huntington.

The expansion of European power and Christianity in the 16th century explained Suleyman's reactive conquest of European territories. By extension, Suleyman as universal caliph of Islam saw as his divine duty to promote the integrity of the faith by rooting out heresy and heterodoxy. His annexation of Islamic territory, such as Arabia, was justified by asserting that the ruling dynasties had abandoned orthodox belief and practice. Each of these annexations was supported by a religious judgment from Islamic scholars as to the orthodoxy of the ruling dynasty.

Suleyman undertook to make Istanbul the center of Islamic civilization. He began a series of building projects, including bridges, mosques and palaces that rivaled the greatest building projects of the world of his

198

time. One of the world's great architects, Sinan, designed mosques that are considered the greatest architectural triumphs of Islam. Suleyman was a great sponsor of the arts and considered one of the great poets of Islam. Under Suleyman, Istanbul became the center of the visual arts, music, literature, and philosophy in the Islamic world. This cultural flowering during the reign of Suleyman represents the most creative period in Ottoman history; almost all the cultural forms that history associates with the Ottomans date from this time.

During the century after the Peace of Westphalia of 1648, two developments of far-reaching importance for the modern world took place in Central and Eastern Europe. The first was the rise of German nationalism in the east, resuming the *Drang nach Osten* (drive to the east). The second was the participation of Russia in the affairs of Europe. The commercial revolution widened the extended markets, which in the west gave rise to the bourgeoisie to exploit labor systematically, and in the east correspondingly strengthened traditional feudal institutions of labor subjugation, such as serfdom.

The three new expanding states of Russia, Austria-Hungary and Prussia inevitably encroached on the three older states: the Holy Roman Empire, which Voltaire ridiculed as neither holy, Roman, nor empire; Poland; and the Ottoman Dominion. Poland was a vast kingdom that extended from east of Berlin to west of Moscow and from the Baltic Sea to the Black Sea.

The differences of the three old states did not exempt them from similar fates of imperialist partition. The rising Western European powers promoted the concept of ethnic nationalism against the titular central authority of the older universal states. Issues of national minorities were twisted to appear as issues national self-determination for the benefit of Western imperialism.

From the beginning of history, size has always been a structural advantage in a competitive environment. "Balkanization" became a word to mean separatist pressure against a large state to break it into small dissenting minor states ripe for new domination by other powers. A balkanization of the former Soviet Union took place on December 26, 1991, that created 15 new nations dominated by the capitalistic West. Yugoslavia was balkanized into seven new nations between 1991 and 1994 that required North Atlantic Treaty Organization intervention to keep peace as the West saw fit.

With all their other differences, the three older universal states had one common characteristic. Each in its own way had an elective structure to yield a central authority over a political realm of diverse ethnic, cultural and religious complexity. The Holy Roman Empire had no standing army after the Peace of Westphalia, having been devastated by the Thirty Years' War and weakened by the tradition of "German liberties" embedded in provincial state sovereignty claimed by more than 300 small German states. The electors at each election required the Holy Roman emperor to accept capitulations to safeguard the feudal rights of the states and religious autonomy. Like the Ottoman Dominion, absolutism in the Holy Roman Empire was decentralized to the local rulers, who did not in turn empower their subjects. The failure of the supreme sovereign to protect the people caused a weakening of popular loyalty to the emperor in the case of the Holy Roman Empire, as it was to the sultan in the case of the Ottoman Dominion.

Poland, like the Holy Roman Empire, did not develop a central authority along absolutist lines, because of the tradition of "Polish liberties" enjoyed by the Polish aristocrats, or *szlachta,* who elected the Polish king. The elective process was even a target of foreign intrigue. Like the Holy Roman Empire, Poland became a political vacuum under stress from centers of high political pressure around Berlin and Moscow.

The Ottoman Dominion was larger than the other two older states and more solidly organized. The Ottoman sultan had a standing army long before any European new monarchy had managed the same. Unlike the Romans, who developed state law, the Ottoman relied on the Koran as the source of Ottoman law. Non-Muslims within the dominion were left to settle their disputes according to the own religious precepts and remained largely outside Ottoman law, but not lawless. The Ottoman weakness was its tolerance, as compared with the absolutism and belligerent theocracy of the new European nation states, not Oriental despotism, as Western historians wrongly claim. Modernity in its distorted form had been polluted by political absolutism from its very beginning.

The history of the world would have been very different had the Kingdom of Poland in the 17th century held together, or the Ottoman Dominion had successfully resisted partition. There would have been no Prussia or Prussian influence in German unification, nor would Russia have become a major Slavic power, nor would the Balkans and Middle East today be fragmented into arenas of European rivalry to become the powder kegs of another future World War in the 21st century. **Very interesting speculation**!

Universal political dominion based on virtue was preempted as the model political institution of modernity by 17th-century imperialist nation-states built on absolutism in the form of new empires, modified subsequently by representative democracy controlled by the propertied class who saw the purpose of civilization as a continuous quest for more property through the enslavement of the world's weak.

This celebration of barbarism as modernity has enslaved four-fifths of the world population into centuries of protracted poverty, produced two World Wars and countless local and regional conflicts, and turned the scientific revolution into an arsenal of weapons of mass destruction that continue to threaten the survival of the human race.

The 19th century was the final century of virtuous Ottomanism. The principal historical factor in Ottoman decline was the hyper-aggressive expansion of European imperialist powers that rose in the age of nation-states that evolved naturally into the age of colonization.

At the beginning of the 17th century, the Ottoman Dominion was still the most powerful universal state in the world outside of China, both in wealth and power. The personal style of governance based on virtue cultivated among the earlier sultans had gradually dissipated. In place of sultanic governance, the bureaucracy ran the Islamic Dominion. Power struggles among the various elements of the bureaucracy - the grand vizier, the *Diwan,* or supreme court, and especially the military, the Janissaries - led to frequent and volatile shifts of political power.

Islamic historians point out that the growth of the bureaucracy and the sultans' uninterest in performing their traditional roles of personifying virtue led to corrupt and predatory local governments, which in turn eroded popular support for the central authority. Western historians point to internal decline in the Ottoman bureaucracy, along with the increased military efficiency of European powers, as the principal reasons for the decline of the Dominion.

A case can be made that Ottoman decline was caused by a loss of virtue as a governing principle. Nevertheless, the decline of virtuous Ottomanism was a gradual and protracted affair lasting more than two centuries. The Ottoman Dominion itself existed nominally as a political entity until World War I, after which it was partitioned out of existence by imperialist European powers. Modernization and revival of a new Ottomanism requires a rediscovery of political virtue, rather than copying the warped model of the imperialistic West.

The process of selecting leaders has plagued all forms of government. Ottomanism believed that the sultan was selected primarily through divine *kut,* a Turkish word meaning "favor". All members of the ruling family had equal claim to the throne. This regal democracy led to the Ottoman practice of royal fratricide to prevent rebellion or rival claims to the throne. Whereas the West labeled this practice as cruel and barbaric, the Ottomans viewed it as a supreme sacrifice required of the ruling family to sustain stability and legitimacy.

In the late 16th century, the Ottoman sultans abandoned this practice of extreme prejudice in favor of primogeniture, possibly because of Western influence. Still skeptical of fraternal loyalty, the brothers of the sultan and the heirs to the throne were locked away in isolation in the palace harem. Some went mad from solitary confinement, but most simply became fat and indolent, addicted to alcohol, drugs, gluttony, sex and aimless leisure. All of them made bad sultans, completely disengaged from governance by virtue. In fact, internecine palace politics, manipulated by foreign interests, often selected new sultans on the basis on their uninterest in government. Instead of Westernizing their succession practice, the Ottomans should have sought their own path of political modernization. In addition, the sultans abandoned the earlier practice of training their heirs to assume the sultanate by providing them with education and leadership training and having them serve in government and the military to gain understanding and experience as effective rulers.

This departure from the vigor of a virtuous sultanate was the prime cause of Ottoman decline, not the sultanate form of government itself as Western historians claimed. It happened also to the absolutist kings of France after Louis XIV, who built Versailles to keep the French royalty and aristocrats in luxury and out of politics. The popular election of leaders, which often yields leaders of political expediency devoid of long-range vision, is also be one of the key weaknesses of the Western democracies.

As a result of the disintegration of the institution of the virtuous sultanate, power went to the Janissaries, the military arm of the government. Throughout the 17th century, the Janissaries slowly took over top military and administrative posts in the government and passed these offices on to their sons, mainly through bribery. Because of this corrupt practice, Ottoman government soon began to be administered by a military feudal class that had little military leadership skills. Under early Ottomanism, position in the government was determined solely through merit. After the 16th century, positions in government were largely hereditary. The quality of the political leadership, the bureaucracy and the military staff declined precipitously.

KUPRILI MEHEMET PASCIA GRAN VIZIR DELL DUE RE OTTOMANNI.

Muhammad Kuprili (1570-1661), as grand vizier, halted the general decline of Ottoman government by rooting out corruption in the imperial government and returned to the traditional Ottoman practice of closely supervising local governments and rooting out local injustice. He also tried to revive the Ottoman universalist practice of protecting Muslim countries from European expansion. This new defensive policy, without the support of an effective military, led to a steady stream of Ottoman military defeats by European powers, which steadily contracted the dominion.

A revived Ottoman threat had produced a coalition of European forces. The Ottomans were forced to accept a 20-year peace in 1664. In 1683, urged on by French instigation, the Ottoman army put Vienna under siege, but was defeated by an alliance of European forces with heavy artillery. King John III of Poland personally led a large army to relieve Vienna and saved Europe from the incalculable consequence of a Turkish foothold in Germany. It was the last victory of Poland before its own partition engineered by the same Austria that the Polish king had saved, with the participation of Prussia and Russia.

During a general withdrawal, the Ottomans had to face a broad counter-offensive composed of forces of the Vatican, Poland, Russia and Venice, joined by the Hapsburgs. It was in this war during the battle between the Venetians and the Turks that the Parthenon in Athens, which had survived intact for 2,000 years, was blown apart as an ammunition dump. While this defeat initiated a long peace between the Ottomans and the Europeans, it also in effect began the steady deterioration of Ottoman control over European territories.

In 1699, the Ottomans were forced to accept the Peace of Karlowitz, which handed over to Austria the provinces of Hungary and Transylvania, leaving only Macedonia and the Balkans under Ottoman control. But the Balkans had begun to destabilize after the Ottoman defeat of 1683. In the 18th century, the Ottomans fought a series of defensive wars against European powers. Between 1714 and 1718, they fought against the small city-state of Venice; between 1736 and 1739, they fought against Austria and Russia in order to stop the expansion of these powers into Muslim territories. The Russians in particular continued to expand aggressively into Muslim territories in Central Asia; these small Muslim states had no place to turn to except to the Ottomans. War with Russia, in fact, dominated the Ottoman scene from much of the 18th century; the two states clashed between 1768 and 1774, and again between 1787 and 1792. In all these wars of the 18th century, there were no clear victors or losers.

European historians tend to view Ottoman decline mainly from the perspective of defeat in wars with Europe. While these wars were significant milestones, Ottoman decline resulted more from economic imperialism that began in the 18th century that led to such defeats in war. Two overwhelming underlying aspects of this decline have also been put forth: meteoric population increase and the failure to industrialize. Yet both of these developments were the results rather than the causes of Ottoman decline.

The 17th and 18th centuries were periods of prosperity in the Ottoman Dominion. As a result, the population of the dominion doubled, which normally would have increased Ottoman power. However, the economic resources of the dominion did not grow with the population increase because of European economic infringement in the form of mercantile imperialism. This eventually led to a massive drain of wealth out of the dominion, causing endemic unemployment and even periodic famine.

The wealth of the Ottomans had largely been due to their strategic presence on trade routes. The Dominion stood astride the crossroads of all the continents and subcontinents: Africa, Asia, India, and Europe. However, European expansion created new trade routes that skirted Ottoman territories. Because the state collected tariffs on all goods passing through the dominion, the economy and the central government lost vast amounts of revenue to new trade routes. What tariffs remained were collected by Europeans who took control of Ottoman customs for the benefit of European economies.

In addition, the Ottomans did not industrialize as the Europeans did in the 18th century. Industrialization principally involved an overhaul of labor practices through the private control of capital and its formation, which accompanied the rise of the bourgeoisie. The Ottoman state, politically a loose dominion and economically based on agriculture and trade, retained centuries-old feudal labor practices, in which production was concentrated in farming and among craft guilds.

Manufacturing did not become a major sector of the Ottoman economy for complex reasons, not the least of which were the reliance on trade flow of goods produced outside the dominion and a shortage of domestic capital needed for industrialization. The shortage of capital was cause by the outflow of wealth through Western imperialism. Increasingly, the economic relationships between the Ottomans and the Europeans evolved into one of imperialistic exploitation, with Europeans buying raw materials at low prices from the Ottomans as part of the privileges granted by "capitulations", and shipping back finished products manufactured in industrialized Europe at great profit, destroying the Ottoman craft industries in the late 18th and early 19th centuries. By the time the Ottomans realized this trade disadvantage, European imperialism was too entrenched to permit belated industrialization in the Ottoman Dominion.

Against the mercantilist policies of the European powers, Ottoman officials clung to an open-free-market policy, the main concern being to provide the home market with an abundant supply of imported commodities and luxuries. The Ottomans mistook mercantilist imports from Europe as tributes that they had traditionally enjoyed for centuries from other nations. Ottoman elites became compradors for foreign interests rather than national industrialists. Unable to formulate a comprehensive protectionist policy for the entire dominion because of its local autonomous structure, the Ottoman sultans allowed the European powers gradually to take control of trade within the Ottoman realm by playing one locality against another, in a race toward the bottom, in much the same way neo-liberalism plays one emerging economy against another today, putting them in the position of competing for the privilege of being exploited at a lower cost.

The character of the "capitulation" tariff concessions originally granted to France by Suleyman as part of his balance-of-power strategy three centuries earlier gradually changed to reduce the Ottoman economy to a dependency of European masters. These treaties of capitulation robbed the Ottomans of their economic independence. With the loss of control of its custom tariffs, the Ottoman Dominion was unable to protect its economy from European mercantilism. Wealth flowed from the Ottoman region into Europe, depriving the local formation of capital needed for industrialization and fueled further advances in European industrialization. European investment and loans in the Ottoman Dominion went only to enterprises that reinforced foreign domination and further reduced the Ottoman state to total financial dependency. The Ottoman Bank, founded in 1856 as a state bank, fell into the total control by English and French capital. Public work and industrial exploitation were financed by foreign capital with all profits flowing abroad and funding only projects that furthered European control.

Ottoman history in the 19th century was dominated by European wars and expansion. The Europeans scrambled for territory throughout the 19th and early 20th centuries, some of which was European territory through inter-European rivalry, but the bulk of which was increasingly outside Western Europe. History had never seen such rapid and frenetic annexation of territory as in the 19th and early 20th centuries by the Western Europeans. A new attitude emerged through the acquisition of non-Western territory in what historians call the New Imperialism, in which the newly subjugated peoples were not absorbed as equals but were considered inferior, notwithstanding their ancient culture and history. The result for the Ottomans was not only the loss of dominion territory and, finally, the demise of the Ottoman dynasty itself, but also an imposed arrest of further development of Ottomanism and its civilization and set it along a path of inevitable decline.

Throughout the non-Western world, anything non-Western was by definition considered by Western cultural hegemony as backward and not modern. Reform and modernization movements in most non-Western systems were conditioned to accept erroneously as a prerequisite to modernization the wholesale rejection of local indigenous culture and tradition, throwing out the timeless good with the obsolete. Modernization was abducted by Western cultural imperialism as Westernization.

But since Westernization is unnatural and inhibiting to indigenous creativeness for non-Westerners, whose instinctive indigenous thought processes and creativeness are systematically and categorically dismissed by Western cultural hegemony, modernization has condemned the non-Western world to centuries of cultural stagnation and de facto inferiority as measured against artificial Western standards. Learned discourses increasingly are conducted only in European languages, making non-Western concepts obscure and difficult to articulate. This was most evident in the two highly sophisticated and cultured living civilizations - the Ottoman/Arab and the Chinese, both of which fell victim to Western political, economic and cultural imperialism at about the same time. Even the culture of ancient Greece was abducted by the West from the Arabs, through whose scholarly translations the West had rediscovered the Greek classics.

Non-Western nationalism was promoted by the Western European new monarchies as a tool to weaken and break up ancient superstates, from the Holy Roman Empire to the Ottoman Dominion to China, not for creating new powerful non-Western states against Western imperialism. Early-20th-century nationalist leaders in both China and Turkey, and in fact the world over, in focusing on political struggles against Western imperialism, unwittingly allowed themselves to be victimized by Western cultural hegemony. They made the serious error of confusing modernity with Westernization, an error from which their successors are not entirely free even today. These nationalist leaders by and large accepted the proposition that the way to resist Western oppression was to out-Western the Westerners, thus setting themselves in a no-win game, and played directly into the hands of the hegemonic West.

Chapter 8 – THE ABDUCTION OF MODERNITY Part 6b: Imperialism and fragmentation

While Western Europe marched steadily toward integration, the non-Western world was, and continues to be, fragmented for easy exploitation in the name of national self-determination.

The British and the French incited the Arabs with pan-Arabism against Ottoman rule, in order to divide the Arab nation into fragmented, weak entities dependent on British and French protection and influence. While Asia and South America are finally moving toward regional integration in the 21st century, albeit still slowly, the Middle East, the Balkans and Africa are still fragmented at the mercy of neo-liberal neo-imperialism led by the United States as the new post-Cold War hegemony. For the non-Western world, resistance to Westernization has yet to be recognized as a prerequisite to true modernization. Globalization of Western culture is the most insidious form of cultural imperialism. What is needed may well be a new Ottomanism of political virtue to rescue the Middle East and the Balkans from perpetual Western domination and exploitation.

The Crimean War (1854-56), like so many of the later Ottoman conflicts with Europe, was instigated not by the Ottomans but by inter-European rivalry. Czarist Russia, Westernized by Peter the Great (1682-1725), was primarily interested in territory as part of a quest for warm-water ports to the Mediterranean Sea. Throughout the 17th and 18th centuries, Russia had been gradually annexing Muslim states in Central Asia. By 1854, Russia found itself edging toward the shores of the Black Sea. Anxious to annex territories in Eastern Europe, particularly the Ottoman provinces of Moldavia and Walachia (now in modern Moldova and Romania), the Russians forced a war on Ottomanism on the pretext that the Ottomans had granted Catholic France, rather than Greek Orthodox Russia, the right to protect Christian sites in the Holy Land, which the Ottomans controlled.

The Crimean War was unique in Ottoman history in that the conflict was not motivated, managed or even influenced by Ottoman policy or interests. The war was a European conflict fought on Ottoman territory, with Britain and France allying with the Ottomans in order to protect their own lucrative economic interests in the region from Russian infringement. The war ended badly for the Russians, with unfavorable terms in the Paris Peace of 1856, but the Ottomans as victors fared even worse. From that point onward, the Ottoman Dominion fell under direct European domination and earned the derisive label as "the sick man of Europe". The Crimean War marked the decline in Ottoman morale and self-respect.

Europeans, for their part, no longer saw the Ottoman state as an equal force as they had three centuries earlier, but as a pliant victim that could be manipulated for larger European purposes. This Eurocentric geopolitics permeated beyond Ottoman territories, throughout the whole world, especially in the final decades of dynastic China.

The imperialist push from Europe, revived after the defeat of Napoleon Bonaparte, took on new economic and racist dimensions. Colonization took on the added objective of developing new markets for manufactured products of European industrialization, and a self-righteous mission of the White Man's Burden. It differed from the current post-Cold-War neo-imperialism of finance capitalism, in which manufacturing is outsourced to low-wage emerging economies through the globalization of finance controlled from New York, but with the equally self-righteous mission of spreading Western democracy to the non-Western world.

After the Napoleonic Wars, which had lasted 22 years until the Congress of Vienna in 1814, war-weariness had permeated throughout Britain and Europe. Throughout that time, only Britain had consistently opposed revolutionary France. Other European nations had been defeated by the French grand armies and/or had signed peace treaties with hitherto invincible Napoleon.

Britain was still recuperating from the huge sacrifice made during the French Wars, which had cost it Stg600 million (British gross domestic product even in 1850, 35 years later, was only Stg570 million). Britain depended on mercantilist trade for survival. Its colonies provided raw materials and a ready market for its manufactured products. Invisible earnings - banking and insurance, what modern economists call factor income - provided rising amounts of incoming cash to the British economy for further industrialization. The two ancient civilizations, the Ottoman Dominion and China, become ideal targets in the British quest for new markets and colonies.

Trade invariably suffered in a shooting war, so Britain adopted gunboat diplomacy. After 1830, Britain became the "Workshop of the World", needing more raw materials to maintain its growing industries financed with new wealth reaped from overseas, and more markets for the finished goods in a mercantilist trade regime. It also needed safe shipping routes. Lord Palmerston (1784-1865) boasted that he wanted only peace and prestige, a euphemism to justify his gunboat diplomacy to expand illegitimate British interests all over the world.

The Opium War (1841) in China, "the sick man of Asia", opened China to Western imperialism. While the British smuggled opium to China from British India, Yankee Clippers from Boston shipped opium from Turkey, grown under British supervision. Much of the profit from opium trade went to Boston and through Boston banks to finance the expansion of the US west.

The war indemnity of the Opium War in 1841 alone imposed on China the payment to Britain of Stg10 million, Stg3 million of which was for the destruction of confiscated opium. The Opium War opened China to five decades of foreign aggression and exploitation, draining wealth on a massive scale from China to Europe and the United States. In 1900, the war indemnity from an Eight-Power Coalition invasion of China as a result of the xenophobic Boxers Uprising forced China to pay 982 million taels (1 tael = 34 grams) of pure silver at the then market price of three taels per pound sterling, yielding Stg327 million, of which Russia received 29 percent, Germany 20 percent, France 15 percent, Britain 11 percent, Japan 7.7 percent and the US 7.3 percent.

Still, this was a mere pittance compared with the profits from systemic economic exploitation of China. This massive drain of silver, coupled with mounting structural economic domination and exploitation, regularly transferred wealth out of China for a century, robbing China of the capital resources needed to modernize, which Westerners blamed instead on China's failure to Westernize her "backward" society.

It was the wealth taken at gunpoint from the non-Western world through imperialism that had fueled the West's modernization, not the Enlightenment, not Western democracy. Westernization was the cause of the non-Western world's demise, not its salvation. Westernization of the non-Western world made resistance to Western gunboat diplomacy ineffective and rendered Western domination a self-fulfilling proposition. This simple fact is still true today - only today, neo-imperialism is called "globalization" and gunboat diplomacy has been replaced with cruise-missile diplomacy.

In Britain, the Reform Bill of 1832 perpetuated the English medieval system of feudal political rights and rejected the new radical ideas of "equality for all" as espoused by the rhetoric of the French Revolution. Instead of the French system of political representation of equal number of voters under the principles of liberty, fraternity and equality, the British held on to the feudal practice of having members of the House of Commons represent land-bound political units such as boroughs and counties, with little regard for population size or for efforts to create equal-size electoral districts. The British suffrage was distributed according to economic substance, reliability and tenure.

The British prided themselves as successful resistors of modernity and identified as their strength an attachment to tradition. Industrialization put British society on a

219

dialectic path toward a worker revolution, as compared with the French Revolution, which was an aristocratic insurrection against the absolute monarchy, taken over by the bourgeoisie through manipulation of peasant discontent with the aristocracy. Had Louis XVI sided with the peasants instead of the aristocrats, France might have ended up as a constitutional monarchy. The Reform Bill diffused revolutionary energy in Britain and provided a mechanism through which social changes could be managed peacefully and accomplished gradually through legal and political means. The secret of Britain's success was its restraint of the rush toward modernity.

Socially progressive laws were only gradually enacted over a period of 15 years, such as the 1833 abolition of slavery within the empire; the Factory Act of 1833 forbidding child labor; the 1835 Municipal Act, which broke up the old landed oligarchies; the Mining Act of 1842 forbidding the use of women and of children under 10 in underground mines; and the Ten Hour Act of 1847. The celebrated liberal John Bright, a Quaker and cotton magnate, attacked the Ten Hour Act as "a delusion practiced on the working classes", citing principles of laissez-faire, free markets, free trade and individual liberty for both employers and workers, in rhetoric similar to that used by neo-liberals today in opposition to the adoption of minimum wages and the regulation against sweatshop conditions. The Ten Hour Act stood, and British industry prospered.

The 1846 repeal of the Corn Laws, which had protected domestic agriculture controlled by the landed gentry, reaffirmed the evolutionary consequences of the Reform Bill by an alliance between factory workers who wanted lower food prices, and their new industrialist employers in support of free trade. Henceforth, free trade became British national policy, and the need for imported food became the popular justification for empire, which was to be upheld by control of the sea by an unrivaled British navy. The Age of the New Imperialism thus was born by transferring British-European feudal systems of privileges overseas to the non-Western World. There was nothing modern about it.

Between 1405 and 1433, a period when China possessed the world's most advanced seafaring technology, the navigator/sailor Zheng He, a Muslim Chinese, explored the seas not for imperialistic expansion but to satisfy the Ming Court's demand for exotic commodities from distant lands. Zheng even brought back from Africa giraffes, ostriches and zebras. Yet the Ming Court abruptly stopped Chinese navigational adventure in 1433, after the death of Zheng. This history baffles Western observers, whose later experience in the West associates navigational adventure with empire-building.

For 28 years (1405-33), Zheng commanded seven fleets that visited 37 countries, through Southeast Asia to faraway Africa and Arabia. In 1420, the Ming navy dwarfed the combined navies of Europe. A great fleet of big ships, with nine masts and manned by 500 men each, set sail in July 1405, almost a century before Christopher Columbus's voyage to America. There were great treasure ships more than 90 meters long and 45m wide, the biggest being 134m long and 57m across, capable of carrying 1,000 passengers. Columbus's Santa Maria was only 26m long. Most of the ships were built at the Dragon Bay shipyard near Nanjing, the remains of which can still be seen today.

Zheng He's first fleet included 27,870 men on 317 ships, including sailors, clerks, interpreters, artisans, medical men and meteorologists, but only a small number of soldiers. On board were large quantities of cargo including silk goods, porcelain, gold and silverware, copper utensils, iron implements and cotton goods and books. The fleet sailed along China's coast to Champa, close to Vietnam and, after crossing the South China Sea, visited Java and Sumatra and reached Sri Lanka by passing through the Strait of Malacca. On the way back, it sailed along the west coast of India and returned home in 1407. Envoys from Calcutta in India and several other countries in Asia and the Middle East also boarded the ships to pay visits to China. Zheng He's second and third voyages taken shortly after followed roughly the same route.

In the autumn of 1413, Zheng He set out with 30,000 men to Arabia on his fourth and most ambitious voyage. From Hormuz he coasted around the Arabian boot to Aden at the mouth of the Red Sea. The arrival of the fleet caused a sensation in the region, and 19 countries sent ambassadors to board Zheng's ships with gifts for Emperor Yong Le. In 1417, after two years in Nanjing and touring other cities, the visiting foreign envoys were escorted home by Zheng. On this trip, he sailed down the east coast of Africa, stopping at Mogadishu, Matindi, Mombassa and Zanzibar and may have reached Mozambique.

The sixth voyage in 1421 also went to the African coast. Loaded with Chinese silk and porcelain, the junks visited ports around the Indian Ocean. Here, Arab and African merchants exchanged spices, ivory, medicines, rare woods, and pearls so eagerly sought by the Chinese imperial court. Zheng He died in the 10th year of the reign of the Ming Emperor Xuande (1433) and was buried in the southern outskirts of Bull's Head Hill (Niushou) in Nanjing. Inscribed on top of the tomb are the Arabic words *"Allahu Akbar"* ("God is Great"). Unlike Columbus and Vasco da Gama, Zheng He did not found any colonies for a Chinese empire. Nor did China turn its seafaring technology into empire-building as the British did in the 19th century.

China never had an empire structure in the Western concept of the term as exemplified by the Roman Empire or the British Empire. Chinese territorial expansion was more along the line of the Ottoman Dominion or the European Union today, with the eager peripheral aspired to join a reluctant center for obvious benefits. Much of the historical expansion of China took place when China was under "Barbarian" occupation, such as the Mongolian Yuan Dynasty and the Manchurian Qing Dynasty. The ruling dynastic houses of "barbaric" origin were inevitably assimilated into Chinese culture, much like the way the Germanic House of Battenberg (Windsor) in Britain adopted British culture.

In this respect, the Chinese Empire was different from the Austro-Hungarian Empire, in which the diverse population was never homogenized and the ruling house remained exclusively Germanic in ethnicity and French in culture. Nor was it similar to the British Empire, for similar reasons. Whenever China was strong and prosperous in history, Chinese foreign policy tended to be isolationist, fending off intruders, rather than expansionist for conquest, as the European new monarchies did. When China became weak and poor in the 19th century from Western imperialism, foreign partition plots took the

223

form of thinly disguised separatism movements. The Ottoman Dominion had many common characteristics with dynastic China.

The concept of Great Powers in geopolitics was formalized during the Congress of Vienna of 1814, which produced a European balance of power among the four European Great Powers - Britain, Russia, Austria and Prussia. France, represented by the great diplomat Talleyrand, exploited the rift between the victors over the Poland-Saxon question to re-enter the diplomatic game as a power in its own right. With Napoleon defeated and the abolition of the Continental System - the precursor of the European Union, with industrialization financed through capitalism at home not for the benefit of the people but for the further enhancement of the propertied class - with no effective rival left for overseas domination, and a virtual monopoly of naval power, Britain embarked on its century of hegemonic superpower predominance, which lasted from 1814 to 1914 and finally deferred to the United States after World War II.

For Britain, the Crimean War was part of the Eastern Question of how to solve the problems posed by the continuing territorial erosion of the Ottoman Dominion, which had been going on since the 1780s and the time of the ministry of Pitt the Younger (1759-1806). To maintain the territorial integrity of the Ottoman Dominion for the purpose of more effectively exploiting its vast resources had become one of the principles of Britain's foreign policy. By the Convention of Balta Liman (1838), Britain had won widespread concessions from the Sublime Porte (French for Sublime Gate), as the Europeans called the Ottoman government, that included special rates on most of the raw materials sold to Britain throughout the Ottoman Dominion, and a host of other benefits, grants, acknowledgements and extraterritoriality, known as capitulations, that gave Britain a very privileged position in the dominion. Unlike the capitulations granted to France as an Ottoman ally against the Holy Roman Empire three centuries earlier; the capitulations granted to Britain were in the form of unequal treaties by a government under duress.

Consequently, Britain felt that it was essential to keep control over the Mediterranean Sea routes and to preserve the Ottoman Dominion as a barrier against further Russian expansion. A similar anti-Russian calculation was central to British opposition to imperialist partition of China. Britain promoted free trade, which favored British national interests, as a universal truth that would lead to world peace and prosperity. The repeal of the Corn Laws in 1846 had set the course of Britain as a free-trade nation.

By encouraging other nations to turn to free trade, Britain was attempting to increase its own wealth and dominance because its economy was more advance in the exploitation of trade and, as Friedrich List has pointed out, that it was the nature of trade that once other nations fell behind in trade, they could never catch up with the hegemonic leader. The British boasted that they had the "secret of civilization" and wanted to export their political and economic system to the rest of the world through a network of local elites acting as compradors for British interest in its colonies and spheres of interest. It is a strategy that the United States inherited after World War II, particularly after the Cold War, in the name of promoting, through trade, allegedly superior American values, vaguely identified as democracy and free-market entrepreneurship.

During this period of European balance of power, the Ottoman sultans hoped to turn their weakness into strength by exploiting inter-European rivalry, a policy that had been successfully practiced by Suleyman three centuries earlier. But with the loss of political and economic independence on the part of the Ottomans under the New Imperialism, such a policy only reduced the Ottoman Dominion deeper into semi-colonial status, further dependent on Franco-British pleasure. The dominion had become much weaker after the loss of territory to Russia, from the separatist creation of new nations dependent on foreign powers within the dominion, and from British and French economic domination. Sultan Abd al-Majid (reigned 1839-61), son and successor of Mahmud II, relied heavily on foreign aid to help him hold the remainder of his dominion together rather than embarking on a struggle of resistance against foreign domination.

In 1799, Muhammad Ali, an Ottoman military officer from the Albanian region, commanded an army in an unsuccessful attempt to drive Napoleon from Egypt. As *pasha* of Egypt after 1805, he was virtually autonomous of his titular overlord, the Ottoman sultan. He westernized his armed forces and administration, created Westernized schools for children of the elite, and began many public works, particularly irrigation projects with foreign loans, to be paid back with resultant agricultural output. The cost of these Westernization reforms weighed heavily on the peasants but brought them few benefits. In 1811, he exterminated the leaders of the Mamluks, who had ruled Egypt almost uninterruptedly since 1250. The Mamluks were a warrior caste dominant in Egypt and influential in the Middle East for more than 700 years. Islamic rulers created this warrior caste by collecting non-Muslim slave boys and training them as cavalry soldiers especially loyal to their owner and each other. They converted to Islam in the course of their training. With his son, Ibrahim Pasha, Muhammad Ali conducted successful campaigns in Arabia against the Wahhabis. In 1820, he sent his armies to conquer Sudan. He scored great successes fighting for the Ottoman sultan in Greece until the British, French, and Russians combined to defeat his fleet at Navarino in 1827.

The sultan, Mahmud II, to secure the intervention of Muhammad Ali in the Greek revolt, had promised to grant him the governorship of Syria. When the sultan refused to hand over the province, Muhammad Ali invaded Syria. In 1839, he rebelled against his Ottoman overlord in Asia Minor, but was forced to desist when he lost the support of France and was threatened by united European opposition, checked by the intervention (1840-41) of Britain, Russia, and Austria. In a compromise arrangement, the Ottoman sultan made the governorship of Egypt hereditary in Muhammad Ali's line. Muhammad Ali retired from office in 1848 because of insanity.

The new Ottoman sultan, Abd al-Majid, was advised by the British to introduce Western reforms. Two decrees (1839, 1856) led to many superficial changes but did not have fundamental or permanent effect. Confident in receiving British and French support, Abd al-Majid in 1853 resisted the Russian claim to act as protector of the Greek Orthodox Christians in the Ottoman Dominion. He had allowed the dominion to weaken because history had shown that a legitimate cause could always get help from a superior source, a cardinal principle of Ottomanism. What he failed to understand was that the New Imperialism was fundamentally indifferent to the Ottoman doctrine of universal virtue and justice. Europe supported the sultan not because it considered it a just cause, but because European powers benefited from such a policy over a despised race.

Russia found the Ottoman Dominion vulnerable in resisting Russian access to the Istanbul Straits - the Bosporus as the West calls it, the Sea of Marmara and the Dardanelles - for easy passage into the Mediterranean. Britain, jealously guarding its mastery of the sea, considered it imperative that Russia must be kept out of the Mediterranean, and the sultan knew it. He continued to play off one European power against another. Russia had shown that it was always going to take any opportunity to probe into Turkish territory; Britain's policy was that the Russians needed firm handling to prevent them from invading Turkey. It was thought that the Russians were not prepared to go to war with Britain over Ottoman territory.

The failure of the 1848 Revolutions turned Europe backward in a retreat from modernity. The balance-of-power diplomacy since 1815 became inoperative as reactionary governments and despotic leaders took hold in Europe, exemplified by Napoleon III in France. Power politics derived from bourgeois dictatorship replaced issues of social justice, political legitimacy and international balance of power.

By 1850, Britain's sensitivity to the Eastern Question increased because India, which had been subjugated and maintained with a mere 75,000 British troops, had become the most important part of the Empire - a key economic asset and the "jewel in the Crown" - as a result of imperialist free trade and overseas expansion. India was a source of raw materials and a populous market, and above all a living demonstration in support of the British superiority complex. Britain feared any threat to the overland rail route to India. A century of the British policy of maintaining the territorial integrity of the Ottoman Dominion on behalf of British interests in the Middle East and the Balkans was shaping up as a conflict to its policy on India.

Napoleon III, the bourgeois Emperor of the French, needed glory through expansionism to uphold the meaning of the "Second Empire", which was ideologically different from the universal monarchist aim of the First Empire. All through the 1840s, the pacifist government of British prime minister George Hamilton Gordon Aberdeen had given Czar Nicholar I the strong impression that Britain would not go to war over the Ottoman Dominion, which encouraged Russia to probe farther south.

In 1815, Britain had been seen in Europe as the principal agent in defeating France militarily, through the successful activities of the Royal Navy and then Arthur Wellesley Wellington's army in the peninsular campaign and later in Europe, economically through providing gold to its allies and supplies to the allied armies and diplomatically through the establishment and maintenance of four anti-Napoleon coalitions. Britain was anxious to enhance its European status after Waterloo and regarded itself as a major force on the international scene. Of all European nations, Britain's political system was the only one that had remained intact throughout the French Wars. Other crowned heads had been removed from their thrones; countries had had their systems of government overturned and replaced, sometimes several times in the period. In Britain, it was felt that only Britain was stable enough to pull Europe together again, because of its conservatism, not its modernity.

Europe was looking to Britain to slow the process of modernization. Britain could not afford to distance itself from Europe because of the proximity of potentially huge markets and the fact that continental instability, particularly the march toward modernity, would adversely impact its domestic affairs.

Britain had adopted the principle of balance of power after the defeat of Napoleon, with itself as first among equals, in an attempt to prevent the domination of Europe by any one other power, and to prevent the march of modernity from again destabilizing Europe. In the past and at various times, different nations had dominated Europe - Spain, France, and Austria-Hungary in particular - with consequences that ended up in war. The Treaty of Paris in 1815 and the settlement at the Congress of Vienna of 1814 ensured that there were no spectacular winners or losers from the French Wars. Britain wanted to maintain the status quo of 1815, not to herald a new modern age. Britain wanted to contain France through cooperation with the other powers. This was a priority in 1815, a policy that was shared by all other European nations.

Later, this policy became a British national prejudice that caused it to fail to note the rise of Prussia. Britain was almost paranoid about a possible replay of French expansionism in the name of modernity, whether it was diplomatic, territorial, economic or through hegemonic influence. Britain tried to keep France pinned down within its borders because France was seen as the most radical and dangerous nation in Europe that could challenge British hegemony. This policy toward France was backward-looking and was maintained for far too long. Even by 1850, the British Foreign Office was still virtually blind to the rise of Prussia, which steadily emerged as a greater threat to the peace and stability of Europe than France. Prussia under Otto von Bismarck was able to delude Britain diplomatically.

In 1875, the Slavic peoples living in the Ottoman provinces of Bosnia and Herzegovina were encouraged by the Western European powers to rise up against Ottomanism. The decline of the Ottomans led two independent, neighboring Slavic states, Montenegro and Serbia, to aid the rebellion. Within a year, the rebellion spread to the Ottoman province of Bulgaria. The rebellion was part of a larger Pan-Slavic movement that had as its goal the unification of all Slavic peoples, most of whom were under the control of Austria, Germany, and the Ottoman Dominion, into a single political unity under the protection of Russia. Anxious also to conquer the Ottomans themselves and seize Istanbul, the Russians allied with the Slavic rebels Serbia and Montenegro and declared war against the Ottomans.

The war went against the Ottomans, and by 1878 they had to sue for peace. Under the peace treaty, the Ottomans had to free all the Balkan provinces, including Bosnia, Herzegovina and Bulgaria. Russia also took substantial amounts of Ottoman territory as "payment" for the war. The Ottomans fell out of the picture, but the Russian victory produced a European crisis over the expansion of Russia. By the early 20th century, the Ottoman Dominion in Europe had receded to a small coastal plain between Edirne and Istanbul. One measure of the losses: before 1850, about 50 percent of all Ottoman subjects lived in the Balkans, while in 1906, the European provinces held only 20 percent of the total.

Foreign wars on the Balkan frontiers, sometimes against the Hapsburgs but especially against Russia, continued to shred Ottoman domains. Within the dominion, many provincial notables during the 18th century had enjoyed substantial degrees of autonomy while acknowledging the titular legitimacy of Ottomanism and the Ottoman state. Seldom, if ever, had rebels sought to break out of or destroy Ottomanism. There had been revolts, but generally these had worked within the Ottoman system, claiming as their goal the rectification of problems within the Ottoman realm, such as the reduction of taxes or restoration of provincial justice. But in the 19th century - in the Balkan, Anatolian, and the Arab provinces alike - movements emerged that actively sought to separate particular areas from Ottomanism and Ottoman rule to establish independent, sovereign states subordinate to no higher political authority, except European protection.

Further, in almost every instance, one or another Western European powers supported the anti-Ottomanism revolts of the 19th century, and Western assistance was crucial to the success of all separatist movements. Thus the 19th century was different in that many of the territorial losses resulted from revolts and rebellions on the part of Ottoman subjects against their suzerain or sovereign occurred with the direct instigation and support of European imperialism.

The 18th century had closed with Napoleon's invasion of Egypt in 1798 to strike at British interests in the Middle East, having successfully evaded Horatio Nelson's fleet to take Malta on the way to Egypt. Napoleon won a brilliant battle over the Mamluks in the Battle of the Pyramids in July 1798. But the invasion was cut short when the French fleet was destroyed by Nelson in Aboukir Bay. Napoleon returned to France in 1799.

In the turmoil, Muhammad Ali eventually seized power in 1805 and established himself as master of Egypt. During his reign (until his death in 1848), Muhammad Ali built up a formidable military that threatened the European balance of power and the Ottomans' hold on the sultanate itself. Egypt embarked on a separate course for the remainder of Ottoman history. It remained the sultan's nominal possession after the British occupation in 1882 but, in 1914, formally became part of the British empire with the Ottoman entry into World War I on the German and Austro-Hungarian side.

At the same moment that Muhammad Ali was seizing control of the southeastern corners of the Ottoman Dominion, the Serbs in the northwestern corner rebelled in 1804. Instead of appealing to the sultan to correct abuses at the hands of the local administration, Serb rebels turned to Russia for aid. A complex struggle involving the two powers and Serb separatists evolved. By 1817, hereditary rule by a Serbian prince had been established and from that date, in reality, Serbia was a state separate from the Ottoman Dominion, falling into the Russian sphere of influence. Legally it became so only in 1878, as a result of the Congress of Berlin. In a sense, this pattern from direct rule to vassalage to independence reversed that of the process of Ottomanism. Other losses derived from the more familiar pattern of war with Russia, ending with a formal agreement, as instanced by the 1812 Treaty of Bucharest that acknowledged the loss of Bessarabia.

The overall pattern in the Balkans was confusing in detail but clear in overall direction. Often a revolt would meet with success with the Russians driving very deep into the southern Balkans. But aroused Western concern, fearful of Ottoman disintegration or Russian success, would convene a gathering to undo the extreme results but allow some losses of Ottoman territory to ensue. The 1829 Treaty of Adrianople typified this pattern. In 1828, Russian armies, while winning major victories in eastern Anatolia, drove down through the western Black Sea areas, through Varna, captured the former Ottoman capital of Edirne on the present-day border of Turkey and Bulgaria and seemed poised to attack Istanbul itself. Nonetheless, despite the decisive victories, Russia yielded up nearly all of its conquests, settling for a few small pieces of land and actual but not formal Ottoman withdrawal from Moldavia and Walachia.

The "Eastern question" continued to be addressed in the manner over the course of the 19th century. On the one hand, many European leaders came to understand the grave risks total Ottoman collapse posed to the general peace held together by a delicate balance of power. Thus they agreed to seek to maintain Ottoman territorial integrity, reversing the potentially devastating results of war at the negotiating table and, in 1856, admitting the Ottoman state into the "Concert of Nations". Thus, the European consensus that the old empire should be maintained, tottering but intact, helped preserve the Ottoman state. The same policy applied to the Open Door policy for China by Western imperialist powers. On the other hand, through their wars and support of the separatist goals of rebellious Ottoman subjects, European powers abetted the very process of fragmentation that they feared and were seeking to avoid. Nationalism was fanned as a weapon only against collapsing empires, not rising ones.

The 1821-30 Greek war of independence clearly illustrates the central role of international geopolitics in the revolts against the sultan. After failing to suppress the Greek rebels, Sultan Mahmut II in 1824 invited Muhammad Ali Pasha to intervene with his powerful navy and army. When the Greek rebellion appeared to be over, in 1827, the combined British, French and Russian fleets annihilated the Egyptian navy at Navarino, and three years later the 1830 Treaty of London forced the Ottomans to acknowledge the formation of a new state, in the southern area of modern Greece.

This sequence of events in turn led to a near takeover of the Ottoman Dominion by Muhammad Ali Pasha. Believing that his help against the Greek rebels entitled him to the Syrian provinces, Muhammad Ali sent his son Ibrahim Pasha against his Ottoman overlord in 1832. Conquering Acre, Damascus, and Aleppo, the Egyptian army won another major victory at Konya in central Anatolia and seemed poised to capture Istanbul (as Russia had been just three years before). In an irony of geopolitics, the Russian nemesis landed its troops between Muhammad Ali's army and Istanbul and became the Ottomans' savior. The century-old foreign foe thwarted a major domestic rebel's intent of overthrowing

Ottoman rule. Fearing that a strong new dynasty leading a powerful state would become its neighbor, the Russians backed the Ottomans and signed the 1833 Treaty of Hunkiar Iskelesi to confirm their protection. The Ottomans fell from the status of a rival to the status of a Russian protectorate.

During the 1830s, Muhammad Ali controlled a section of southeast Anatolia and most of the Arab provinces and, in 1838, threatened to declare his own independence. The Ottomans attacked his forces in Syria, but were crushed and again rescued, this time by a coalition of Britain, Austria, Prussia and Russia (but not France). These clashes stripped Muhammad Ali of all his gains - Crete and Syria as well as the Holy Cities of Mecca and Medina - leaving him only hereditary control of Egypt as compensation.

The lesson seemed clear. The Western powers were unwilling to permit the emergence of a dynamic and powerful Egyptian state that threatened Ottoman stability and the international balance of power. Muhammad Ali did not become the master of the Middle East in significant measure because the European states would not allow it. Much of current US policy toward Iraq can be understood in a similar light.

The severance from the Ottoman state of its Egyptian province entered a final phase in 1869, when the Egyptian ruler, the Khedive Ismail, presided over the opening of the Suez Canal under British protection, with the world premiere of Giuseppe Verdi's "Aida". The canal brought British occupation of the province by 1882. Britain declared a protectorate over Egypt in 1914, nearly four centuries after the armies of Sultan Selim I had entered Cairo and incorporated the Mamluk empire into the Ottoman Dominion.

The Eastern Question revealed the diplomacy after the Ottoman-Russian war of 1877-78 that triggered major territorial losses for the Ottomans. In the first round of negotiations, Russia forced the Ottomans to sign the Treaty of San Stefano, creating a gigantic zone of Russian puppet states in the Balkans reaching to the Aegean Sea itself. Such a settlement would have vastly enlarged the Russian area of dominance and influence and destroyed the European balance of power.

Bismarck, the German chancellor who was the leading statesman of the age and in history, and who after 1871 had feared that another European war would jeopardize the new German Empire, proclaimed himself an "honest broker" seeking peace and no territorial advantage for Germany and convened the Powers in Berlin. There the assembled diplomats negotiated the Treaty of Berlin, which took away most of the Russian gains and parceled out Ottoman lands to other treaty signatories as door prizes. Serbia, Montenegro and Romania all became "independent" states under Austrian protection. Bosnia and Herzegovina were lost in reality to Hapsburg administration but remained nominally Ottoman, until their final break in 1908, when they were annexed by Austria. The Greater Bulgaria of the San Stefano Agreement was reduced, one-third becoming independent and the balance remaining under qualified and precarious Ottoman control. Romania and Russia settled territorial disputes between them, with the former obtaining the Dobruja mouth of the Danube and yielding southern Bessarabia to Russia in exchange. Other provisions included the cession to Russia of pieces of eastern

Anatolia and to Britain the island of Cyprus, a strategic naval base to protect the Suez Canal and lifeline to India. France was appeased by being allowed to occupy Tunis.

The Treaty of Berlin in 1878 shows the hegemonic power of Europe over the whole world during the last part of the 19th century, able to impose its wishes on the world with little resistance from non-Europeans, drawing lines on maps and deciding the fate of peoples and nations with impunity for the benefit of Europeans. It would do so again on many more major occasions - for example, partitioning Africa in 1884, the near-partition of China and the partition of the Middle East and the Balkans after World War I.

With historic consequences, the peoples of both Western Europe and the non-Western partitioned lands falsely concluded that military strength/weakness implied cultural, moral and religious strength/weakness. The victims were brainwashed to believe that their failure to modernize their armed forces was the result of their cultural backwardness and as such had brought them a deserved fate of foreign domination. Western barbarism is misconstrued as modernization, and Westernization is seen to have been ordained as the only path to modernization for the non-Western world, rather than the cultural suicide that it actually was. The fateful history of oligarchic Sparta's conquest over Athens, the model of Greek democracy, during the Peloponnesian War, which set Western civilization on the wrong path, has been repeated globally age after age, all the way into modernity.

Chapter 9 – Pulling It All Together

As promised, here I want to pull it all together for you. I know reading Liu's rather lengthy "walk through history" may have become tedious but in the end I sincerely hope you found it enlightening and rewarding.

Whether you are westernized or easternized, an occidental or oriental, Arab, or whatever, it is safe to assume that you view the world around you through your own eyes, the way you were raised, from the influences in your life, etc.

Liu's attempt to describe the history of world affairs was magnificent; however, Liu's heritage is Chinese and his treatise is wrought with oriental bias.

What I want you to see here is this: Liu's treatise described many things but what transcends all cultural and socio-economic boundaries is the fact that economics and/or "massive consumption" are largely the main reason behind many of the world's problems then as well as today.

Now I want you to view the world of YOU through the same socio-economic/massive consumption eyes taking into account how over consumption has affected your life completely.

I am a scientist, a Christian and much more and my beliefs, education and training slants me in various directions in my thoughts and especially how I view the world around me. You are no different. Everyone has a personal bias.

But all of the above goes away when I view my life as a consumer of goods and services and look for the effect of consumption on my life.

I consume too much; I give little back in exchange. I learned that less is actually more. I will get into this further later on.

First I want to present an article I found from "A Slice of Infinity" written by Andy Bannister, who is a member of the speaking team at Ravi Zacharias International Ministries in Toronto, Canada.

Aren't All Religions Equally Valid?

One of the most common accusations flung at Christians is that they are arrogant. "How can you believe that you're right and Hindus, Buddhists, Muslims—all the thousands of other religions—are wrong?" Isn't it the height of arrogance to claim that Jesus is the way to God? A way, possibly. But the way?

This issue haunts many Christians and makes us reluctant to talk about our faith. We don't want to appear arrogant, bigoted, or intolerant. This pluralistic view of religions thrives very easily in places like Canada or Europe where tolerance is valued above everything else. It's very easy slip from the true claim—"all people have equal value"—to the false claim that "all ideas have equal merit." But those are two very different ideas indeed.

Let's take a brief look at the "all religions are essentially the same" idea. Suppose I say that I've just got into literature in a big way. This last year, I've read William Shakespeare, Virginia Woolf and Tolkien, but also Harry Potter and The Very Hungry Caterpillar—and I've concluded that every author is identical. Would you conclude that: (a) this is the most profound statement on literature you've ever heard? Or would you conclude (b) that I don't have the first clue what I'm talking about? I suggest that you'd probably choose (b). Now, what about the statement "all religions are the same"? Doesn't it likewise suggest that the person making it hasn't actually looked into any of them? Because once you do, you realize it's not that most religions are fundamentally the same with superficial differences but the reverse is the case: most religions have superficial similarities with fundamental differences.

A further problem with the idea that all religions are essentially the same is that it ignores a fundamental truth about reality: ideas have consequences. What you believe matters, because it will effect what you do. To claim that all religions are essentially the same is to say that it

242

doesn't matter what you believe as long as you're sincere—and this neglects the fact that you can believe something sincerely and be sincerely wrong. Hitler held his beliefs with sincerity—that doesn't make them true.

However, truth, by its very nature, is exclusive. If it is true, as Christianity claims, that Jesus was crucified, died, and rose from the dead, then it is not true, as Islam claims, that Jesus never died in the first place and that somebody else was killed in his place. Both claims cannot be true. Truth is exclusive.

But just because truth is exclusive, that doesn't make truth cold and uncaring. Truth for the Christian is personal. The Jesus who said "I am the only way" also said "I am the truth." In other words, ultimate truth is not a set of propositions but a person. As the Bible says in 2 Timothy 2:12, "I know whom I have believed." Not what I have believed or experienced but whom. Jesus Christ.

To ask why we think that Jesus Christ is the only way is to miss the point entirely. Jesus does not compete with anybody. Nobody else in history made the claims he did; nobody else in history claimed to be able to deal with the problems of the human heart like he did. Nobody else in history claimed, as he did, to be God with us. To say that we believe Jesus is the only way should have nothing to do with arrogance and everything to do with introducing people to him.

My purpose in presenting you with the article above was to give you a glimpse into how to actually view anything and how to reason out to an educated conclusion something that is a problem. In other words, use your intellect to discern rather than emotions. Always be aware of your personal bias. When you hear or read news, pull it apart, look for what is there but what isn't obvious.

Example: In the news recently was the killing of the black youth Treyvon Martin by Neighborhood watch suspect George Zimmerman. The public sentiment against this man notwithstanding, in any situation there is more than being said and more that will come out in the subsequent investigation; however, Zimmerman is already being castigated as guilty when all of the facts are still to be discovered. Don't fall prey to public opinion. Do your own thinking and do it intellectually rather than emotionally.

Earlier I said that less is actually more. I have learned that by giving I get, by sacrificing, I gain. This is opposite of what our society teaches in over consumption. Everyone is in a rush to acquire "stuff" but with all this stuff comes responsibility...where do you put it, how do you protect it, insure it, store it, use it?

I have learned that over-acquisition of goods and services actually lead to a loss of goods and services by the sheer weight of responsibility of holding onto my "stuff".

Many years ago I was a fanatic for old Mercedes automobiles and had an extensive collection worth a good amount of money. Looking back at how much time, money, and effort was required to maintain my collection actually brings almost nausea on my part. I can remember to this day, when I sold the whole collection, the feeling of relief to be rid of its burden.

My point: examine your own life and determine where over/massive consumption is damaging your life. Look and dig deeper into world problems looking for the socio-economic causes to better understand what is happening around you.

Open your eyes to massive consumption and "just say no" to acquiring more stuff. Give more than you take and watch the blessings come pouring in.

I Have a Special Gift for My Readers

I appreciate my readers for without them I am just another author attempting to make a difference. If my book has made a favorable impression please leave me an honest review. Thank you in advance for you participation.

My readers and I have in common a passion for the written word as well as the desire to learn and grow from books.

My special offer to you is a massive ebook library that I have compiled over the years. It contains hundreds of fiction and non-fiction ebooks in Adobe Acrobat PDF format as well as the Greek classics and old literary classics too.

In fact, this library is so massive to completely download the entire library will require over 5 GBs open on your desktop.

Use the link below and scan all of the ebooks in the library. You can select the ebooks you want individually or download the entire library.

The link below does not expire after a given time period so you are free to return for more books rather than clog your desktop. And feel free to give the link to your friends who enjoy reading too.

I thank you for reading my book and hope if you are pleased that you will leave me an honest review so that I can improve my work and or write books that appeal to your interests.

Okay, here is the link…

http://tinyurl.com/special-readers-promo

PS: If you wish to reach me personally for any reason you may simply write to mailto:support@epubwealth.com.

I answer all of my emails so rest assured I will respond.

Meet the Author

Dr. Leland Benton is Director of Applied Web Info, a holding company for ePubWealth.com, a leading ePublisher company based in Utah. With over 21,000 resellers in over 22-countries, ePubWealth.com is a leader in ePublishing, book promotion, and ebook marketing.

As the creator and author of "The ePubWealth Program," Leland teaches up-and-coming authors the ins-and-outs of today's ePublishing world. He has assisted hundreds of authors make it big in the ePublishing world.

Leland also created a series of external book promotion programs and teaches authors how to promote their books using external marketing sources.

Leland is also the Managing Director of Applied Mind Sciences, the company's mind research unit and Chief Forensics Investigator for the company's ForensicsNation unit. He is active in privacy rights through the company's PrivacyNations unit and is an expert in survival planning and disaster relief through the company's SurvivalNations unit.

Leland resides in Southern Utah.

Visit some of his websites
http://www.AddMeInNow.com
http://www.AppliedMindSciences.com
http://www.BookbuilderPLUS.com
http://www.BookJumping.com
http://www.EmailNations.com
http://www.EmbarrassingProblemsFix.com
http://www.ePubWealth.com
http://www.ForensicsNation.com
http://www.ForensicsNationStore.com
http://www.FreebiesNation.com
http://www.HealthFitnessWellnessNation.com
http://www.Neternatives.com
http://www.PrivacyNations.com
http://www.RetireWithoutMoney.org
http://www.SurvivalNations.com
http://www.TheBentonKitchen.com
http://www.Theolegions.org
http://www.VideoBookbuilder.com

**Some Other Books You May Enjoy From
ePubWealth.com, LLC Library Catalog**

EPW Library Catalog Online
http://www.epubwealth.com/wp-content/uploads/2013/07/Leland-benton-private-turbo.pdf

EPW Library Catalog Download
http://www.filefactory.com/f/562ef3ea1a054f0a